LASTING IMPACT

Every Day is a Bonus Day!

Blessings,

Josh

6/2021

LASTING IMPACT

JOHN MIKSA

WITH SCOTT P. LEARY, M.D.

MY MIRACULOUS RECOVERY FROM TOTAL PARALYSIS

TATE PUBLISHING
AND ENTERPRISES, LLC

Published by Tate Publishing & Enterprises, LLC
127 E. Trade Center Terrace | Mustang, Oklahoma 73064 USA
1.888.361.9473 | www.tatepublishing.com

Tate Publishing is committed to excellence in the publishing industry. The company reflects the philosophy established by the founders, based on Psalm 68:11,
"The Lord gave the word and great was the company of those who published it."

Published in the United States of America

ISBN: 978-1-63063-931-0
1. Biography & Autobiography / Personal Memoirs
2. Biography & Autobiography / General
14.07.01

For Sheri, my wife and best friend

ACKNOWLEDGMENTS

No one can endure and recover from such a devastating accident without the help of many people. Some may be just ordinary citizens. Others may have spent decades studying and perfecting their medical talents in preparation to help those in time of their desperate need. By the grace of God, all such people, far too many to list here, came into my life at exactly the right time and place. Although there were many doctors, nurses, specialists, and technicians involved in my case, I would be remiss to not give special thanks to Dr. Leary, my neurosurgeon. In addition to performing my miraculous surgery, Scott has become a friend for life. To him and everyone involved in my case, I thank each and every one of you from the bottom of my heart.

I especially want to thank Meg and Wes Wright, my daughter and son-in-law, for their unwavering support and continuous prayers during this extraordinary period. Also, I am thankful to Matt and Kelly Miksa, my son and daughter-in-law, who remained in constant contact with Sheri during my hospitalization. I must also thank all my relatives and friends who reached out to Sheri and me and filled us with encouragement and hope. Finally, I want to express my deepest thanks and sincerest love to Sheri, who stayed by my side during my darkest hour, never gave up hope, and refused to believe in anything except a happy ending.

CONTENTS

Part I: The Accident

Part II: The Surgeries

Part III: The Miraculous Recovery

Part IV: The Circle Is Now Complete

FOREWORD

When I first met John Miksa, he was in a full neck brace, holding a bag of blue and red polo shirts.

To be honest, he was a sight to behold: a tall, lean man with a smile that stretched from ear to ear, despite what had clearly been some damage to his neck or spine.

I introduced myself, shook his hand, met his wife, Sheri, and then heard his incredible story. From the brink of death to miracle surgery to inspiring rehabilitation, the challenges John had overcome in just a few short weeks were more than most will face in a lifetime.

On this particular day, John and his wife were making the rounds, personally thanking all who had been involved with his care: his surgeon and surgical team, recovery room and intensive care teams, doctors, nurses, physical and occupational therapists, and even me, the CEO. The polo shirts were gifts from him and Sheri to those who had played a role in his healing and recovery. They read, "John's Team, 8-21-09, Part of a Miracle."

But as proud as I am of the outstanding care John received at Scripps Health, his story is more than a tale of surgical procedures and rehabilitation. John's extraordinary rise from the ashes is equally about the power of attitude, determination, and zest for life. His caregivers will tell you they saw this in John when he was brought into our trauma bay, when he learned to walk again in our rehabilitation center, and when he walked out of the hospital on his own, just weeks later to a new lease on life.

Almost one year from the day when John was transferred by ambulance to another Scripps location, he gathered once again with friends, doctors, and other caregivers, this time on their bikes. In a celebratory ride from the hospital where he had his surgery to the hospital where he underwent two weeks of intensive inpatient rehabilitation, John shared his personal recovery milestone and helped us all find healing along the way.

We all face challenges and pain in our lives, and sometimes, it feels like there is no coming back. John's inspirational story provides hope for a new beginning. It reminds us that we all have choices, that life goes on, and that how we choose to live is up to us.

—Chris Van Gorder, FACHE
President and CEO
Scripps Health

INTRODUCTION

Every so often, a seminal event occurs. Something that is wildly fantastic and entirely unpredictable. Many times, these events are referred to as miracles. Miracles, by definition, defy logic and transcend scientific reason. Such events surpass all known human powers and eclipse the laws of nature. They are supernatural.

As a neurosurgeon, I am privileged to play a role in what many of my patients refer to as their miracles. From a very early age, I knew I wanted a career in medicine. I felt driven to be a difference maker in people's lives. After exploring many surgical disciplines in my first year of medical school at Washington University in St. Louis, my path was clear. No specialty afforded a physician the opportunity to change people's lives like neurosurgery. I was fascinated with the challenges neurosurgery presented. Horrifying injuries with devastating permanent neurologic deficits and incurable brain tumors became a daily reality.

I've had my share of remarkable success stories. Many patients have regained the use of their arms and legs or had a brain or spinal tumor removed without complications under my care. Neurosurgical procedures are incredibly stimulating, invigorating, and intense. The margins for error are razor thin. The judgment needed to decide what to do, and when to do it, can be daunting. Mistakes in judgment or technique result in devastating consequences. You only get one swing.

Spinal cord injuries are rampant across America and in the world. It is estimated that approximately 12,000 to 20,000 new cases of spinal cord injury occur in the United States each year. Most cases involve an automobile accident. Depending on the extent of neurologic damage, spinal cord injuries are classified as either incomplete or complete. The majority of injuries are considered incomplete, meaning that there is still a measure of preserved function, motor or sensory, below the level of injury. The most severe cases are classified as complete, meaning that *all* neurologic function has been lost.

On that fateful day in August 2009, I examined John Miksa in the trauma suite at Scripps Memorial Hospital in La Jolla, California. Like so many others before him, John had been rendered a complete quadriplegic after being violently struck by a car while riding his bike. It was a shocking turn of events. Even though he had no associated head injury and his mental state was clear, it was still difficult for John to grasp the magnitude of the situation. His presentation was very extreme. He had a 100 percent complete acute spinal cord injury. He had no feeling below his upper chest. He could barely move his shoulders and biceps but nothing else. He could not move his fingers, hands, or legs even the slightest bit. He had no rectal tone and flaccid reflexes. And even more concerning, he was in florid spinal shock. Because of the severe trauma to his spinal cord, he not only lost his voluntary nerve function, but he also lost involuntary nerve function. As a result, his blood pressure was crashing and his heart was abruptly slowing down, a deadly combination.

MRI and CT scans revealed multiple spinal injuries, and for the first time, to the trained eye, provided a glimmer of hope. Many patients with severe trauma to the cervical spine have dislocation of the vertebrae and transect the spinal cord, an irreversible condition. While John did have fractures in his neck, the main concern was a massive acute ruptured disc that was smashing his spinal cord into oblivion.

At this stage, the medical decision making became highly complicated. Typically, a patient with a complete spinal cord injury does not benefit from emergent surgery because the damage is permanent. Furthermore, John was medically unstable due to spinal shock. Despite these overwhelming odds, it was clear that an emergent procedure to decompress his spinal cord and stabilize his cervical spine was imperative. If there was any chance for even a partial recovery, the surgery could not wait. If surgery were delayed, the outcome would be sealed: permanent quadriplegia and a lifetime in a wheelchair. I quoted John a less than 1 percent chance of any form of recovery.

I was not confident the surgery would change anything. The damage appeared too extensive and too severe. But I thought it was worth a shot, and I hoped to convince John and his wife to let me proceed.

—Scott P. Leary, MD
Board Certified Neurosurgeon
San Diego, California

Fellowship Trained
Complex Spine Surgery

Chair, Spine Committee
Scripps Memorial Hospital
La Jolla, California

PROLOGUE

The weather is perfect. The wind is down, and the sky is a brilliant blue peppered with a few pure white clouds and some gracefully gliding seagulls. I can see the car approaching, coming from the opposite direction at about 25 mph. I'm in the bike lane going up a slight grade at 18 mph. To keep my pace, I stand up and pedal out of the saddle, which allows me to see clearly the only moving car sharing this quiet neighborhood road.

My ride has taken me so close to the Pacific Ocean that I can smell the salty air. Everything is the way it should be. My mind shifts its focus back to the task at hand—getting to the top of the grade while keeping my cadence and maintaining my speed.

Suddenly, without warning, the car turns directly into my path. I am absolutely stunned. Moments before, the car was heading north as I rode south. It was supposed to go past me like thousands of others had done during countless previous rides. Instead, it is headed right for me as if drawn to my bike by some powerful magnetic force.

I have no time to avoid it and nowhere to go. My pedaling stops as I'm overcome with astonishment and drenched with fear. This just cannot be happening. The car is not stopping! I yell at the top of my voice, "*No! Stop! No!*" Everything shifts into slow motion.

In a fraction of a second, my life is about to change dramatically.

PART I

THE ACCIDENT

BIKE VS. CAR—BIKE LOSES

It was August 2009. Sheri, my wife, and I were enjoying the last week of a visit from Meg, our daughter, and her husband, Wes. They had spent the last five years in Spain as missionaries for Cru and had recently moved back to Austin, Texas. Thankfully, they had decided to drive out to Carlsbad, California, and spend a few weeks with us.

To top off their visit, we chose to drive to Las Vegas for a three-night stay. While there, we thoroughly enjoyed ourselves walking the Strip and touring the inside of the mega-hotels. We especially enjoyed the buffet at the hotel where we stayed—in fact, a bit too much. I was sure my caloric intake had exceeded those I'd burned while walking around the city in spite of the brutally hot weather. As soon as we returned home, my scale confirmed my suspicions. Indeed, "What's eaten in Vegas doesn't necessarily stay in Vegas!"

Determined to shed the unwanted weight, I decided that getting back on my bike, a 2004 Specialized™ Roubaix, would be the best way to peel away the extra pounds I'd gained. Since I'd taken up cycling again five years ago, I had progressively added more miles each week. In fact, before Meg and Wes had arrived, I'd been logging between 150 to 200 miles a week.

Now, although I was eager to get back on the bike, I knew my family was far too busy for me to go off on one of my fifty-mile bike rides, especially Thursday, our first full day back from Vegas. Meg and Wes were getting ready to drive back to Texas in two days, on Saturday, August 22. Then, on Friday, they spontaneously decided to run errands, get some supplies, and enjoy one last day of perfect Carlsbad weather. I sprung at the chance to squeeze in an easy twenty-two-mile ride.

My planned route was one I had taken many times before—I left the house, headed due west for the Pacific Ocean, and then made a right turn to ride north up the coast. It was a perfect day for a ride, although I knew we were in the height of tourist season, which always presented its own set of challenges for cyclists. The main issue stemmed from out-of-town drivers unfamiliar with the sporting activities surrounding them as they drove. If you add smartphone texting, tweeting, and Web surfing, you have a potentially deadly mix of distracted drivers and vulnerable walkers, runners, and cyclists.

I knew all of this. When you love cycling as much as I do, though, you weigh the risks, take all the appropriate precautions, and then get moving. Just fifty days earlier, I had done this very thing. I had set out for a twenty-mile ride that took me parallel to the Pacific Ocean heading south on the Pacific Coast Highway (PCH). As was often the case, my final destination was a Starbucks, where I planned to rendezvous with Sheri, throw my bike in the back of the SUV, enjoy a soy latte, and drive home.

That hot July day, I was about four miles from meeting her as I approached a red light across from the park. I slowed down just enough so the light would turn green before I got to it. Once there, I quickly pulled alongside the lead car going about 24 mph, across from its right rear panel. Then, without warning, the driver made a right turn in front of me, forcing me to squeeze as hard as I could on my brakes.

Unfortunately, I ran out of room and could not stop in time. As he abruptly made his turn into an angled parking space, my front wheel struck his back right tire and down I went. I had slowed to about 10–12 mph by the time he hit me. I tried breaking my fall with my right hand, but instead, my ribs cushioned the fall. Although none were broken, my ribcage was sore for a month.

Thank God for helmets. Although mine cracked in two places, it spared me a concussion. My bike got the worst of it, and I was certain it was out of commission for good. Meanwhile, Sheri was waiting for me to ride up to our SUV in the Starbucks parking lot. Instead, when she picked up her phone, my shaky voice informed her, "I was hit by a car and I'm not sure if I can ride the rest of the way to meet you."

Sheri, always the essence of calm, replied, "Stay where you are. I'll be there in five minutes." However, I knew she was frightened because I had to tell her twice that I'd been hit by a car. She just couldn't absorb it the first time. By the time she arrived, the paramedics had looked me over and asked me if I wanted to go to the hospital. Since I only had a few scrapes, a sprained wrist, and some sore ribs, I declined. While not physically injured, the young surfer who hit me seemed more shaken by the accident than I was. I give him credit for staying at the scene and providing his contact and insurance information.

Although it wasn't as calamitous as it could have been, the accident did heighten my awareness of the dangers of cycling among cars in our area. It didn't matter that I always obeyed the traffic laws and dutifully used every bike lane I could find. Distracted drivers are just that—distracted—and I now realized, as never before, how risky cycling could be in traffic.

There's a saying among cyclists: "You either *have* crashed or you are *going* to crash." Now, at least, it appeared I could check off that box! In fact, because my crash involved a car, I figured this had more karma points than simply falling off my bike or running into another cyclist. This was as close to getting hit by lightning and living to tell about it, right? Although I told myself there was no way this could ever happen again, I vowed to be even more vigilant. Lightning would not strike *me* twice!

Now, nearly two months later, I was ready to set out for an easy twenty-two-mile ride. It was time to burn off some of those Vegas calories. The kids were off doing their own thing, anxious about their very long drive home to Texas, and Sheri was multitasking as only she could.

I often describe Sheri as having only two speeds: on and off. According to her mother, she has been this way her whole life. This is the same woman who left a cushy lifestyle in Bellevue, Washington, halfway through her junior year in high school to move to Anchorage, Alaska, to live with her father and brother in a modest cabin on the side of a mountain. There was no running water, no electricity, and a primitive bathroom. Undaunted, this strawberry blond, blue-eyed young woman of Scandinavian descent adapted to her new environment, graduated high school with honors, and became a runner-up in the Miss Alaska pageant. She went on to finish her undergraduate degree while working for ARCO in Prudhoe Bay, Alaska, located above the Arctic Circle! Eventually, she became the manager of ARCO's 1,900-bed housing facility for its Prudhoe Bay workers.

Still, Sheri had loftier goals for her career, which led her to graduation from the Stanford Graduate School of Business with an MBA. Since then, Sheri has held numerous senior executive and CEO positions in the foodservice industry and has become known for her turnaround skills. Seemingly married to her career, I count myself very fortunate that she fell in love with me, and we married in 1996. I could not ask for a more loving, trustworthy, nonjudgmental, and steadfast partner—qualities that were about to serve us both very well.

Sheri had agreed to meet me at a local Starbucks, after I completed my ride, which I had expected to be at about 3:00 p.m. We would enjoy our usual latte of choice, catch up on each other's day, and drive the last two miles home. That night, we had planned for a send-off barbeque with Meg and Wes, knowing they were beginning their drive back to Texas the next morning.

With everyone focused on their own activities, it presented a perfect chance to sneak in an early Friday afternoon ride. So I geared up, did all my pre-ride checks, said my usual pre-ride prayers, made the sign of the cross, and started on my way. The first half mile of this route always presented a challenge because the grade was above 10 percent. I tended to sense how a ride would feel each time I took off based on how I felt going up this stretch. Some days, I felt like attacking it, but on other days, I just wanted to find my legs and lumber up to the stoplight at the top of the hill. Today was one of those lumber days after too much buffet ballast.

The next one and a half miles quickly made up for any slight pain I experienced. I always enjoyed keeping a nice cadence on this section and going over 30 mph. What a great feeling to fly down a slight hill in an aerodynamic tuck, with the wind whooshing through your helmet. Every time I took this route, I was reminded why I took up cycling. It was absolutely exhilarating!

What I wasn't thinking about were the very thin tires I was riding on that were making exceptionally narrow contact with the road. Nor did I think about my daily problems or about unleashed aggressive dogs or distracted drivers. Instead, I was immersed in the moment, marveling at how something could feel so good while being so good for my health.

Even as a kid growing up in the Tampa Bay area, playing sports year-round, being in shape seemed to be a natural part of my life. When one sports season ended, my buddies and I would just switch to the next ball. As I got older and overtaken with life's responsibilities, it became harder to stay active and in decent shape. Our move in 2002 to Carlsbad, California, presented a perfect opportunity to embrace a more active lifestyle. At first, I combined gym workouts with golfing. But when I turned fifty, I knew I needed to do more. That is when I put my clubs in storage and got on my bike and started to burn thousands of calories per ride.

At the corner of Poinsettia and Avenida Encinas, I was always presented with a choice. I could go a quarter of a mile farther west and then head north on PCH or I could turn right and avoid more tourists. I decided that if the light was green, I would maintain my cadence and speed and head for PCH. If the light turned red, I would turn right. The light was red this day, so I turned.

About five miles away from home, I came to another red light at Palomar Airport road. I pulled up to the front in the straight-ahead lane and found myself next to a pickup truck in the left turn lane. The driver had his windows down and we had a minute or two before the light would turn green. He complimented me on my bike, which I had just cleaned and polished before my ride, and I asked him if he rode. He said, "Yes, but not enough." Then, I encouraged him to ride more, and he, in turn, told me to enjoy the rest of my ride and to be safe.

The light turned green, and off I went. In just a few miles my route eventually put me onto PCH, heading north along the ocean. As I rode through Carlsbad, I spotted the usual frolicking dogs, but riding north put me on the other side of the road from the pets. No unleashed chasers to contend with today!

Up through Carlsbad I went, past the Army/Navy School, and into Oceanside. Then, once on Cassidy Street, it was only a few hundred yards to turn right onto Pacific Street and head north toward Oceanside Pier. Because it was Friday afternoon in late August, I knew this part of my route could become a bit dangerous. The beach here was popular, and more than once, I'd found myself in a close call with a surfer removing their long board from their car, eager to catch the next great wave. If you were passing them at that moment, it could be hazardous to your health. Cyclists tended to be extra careful riding through this area.

Once past the Oceanside Pier, it was clear sailing to the end of Oceanside Harbor. From there, I knew it was twelve miles to get home. To get to Starbucks, where I would meet Sheri, was just ten miles. Usually, I would stop at the loop at the end of the harbor, pull out my cell phone, and give Sheri a call. But today would be an easy, relatively short ride. I reasoned that I was only about thirty minutes away from meeting her, and I hadn't been gone much longer than that. Besides, she would be doing three things at once, anyway. So with that in mind, I decided to keep cycling and not stop to call her.

Little did I know that this decision would put me on a timeline for a rendezvous with my destiny.

Leaving the harbor loop, I could tell that my body was recovering from the Vegas trip and was beckoning me to go faster. I wanted to keep my heart rate under 120 bpm, though, so I resisted the urge to accelerate as long as I could. Finally, just eight miles from meeting Sheri, I decided to crank it up a notch. At this point, going south on Pacific Street, it was easy to go over the 25 mph speed limit because of the slight downward slope of the road. However, the speed limit is there for good reason—a pedestrian crosswalk connects a popular food shack on the east side of the road to the beach on the west side right at the bottom of the grade. To encourage adherence to the 25 mph limit, a radar-activated speed readout flashes at vehicles and bikes before they get to the crosswalk.

Determined not to violate the 25 mph restriction, I was pleased when the sign flashed "21" to indicate my speed as I approached. I proceeded through the pedestrian crossing and continued south up the slight grade on Pacific Street. I stood up to pedal and kept my pace at about 18 mph—another great ride amidst another picture-perfect day.

And then, it happened. Abruptly and without warning, the driver of a car heading north in the opposite direction turned directly into my path. What seemed like a harmless car just moments ago became a deadly juggernaut heading right for me. I felt shocked, angered, dumbfounded, cornered, frightened, and helpless. This could not be happening to me—not again!

Amazingly, I managed to yell as loud as I could, "*No! Stop! No!*" But it was too late—I was out of time and out of space. My bike, the car, and everything around me went into slow motion. My eyes became riveted on the car's grill. It looked like a wall with teeth, about to crush me. As the car continued its angled path toward me, blocking any possible escape, I knew it was going to break my left ankle, probably my left leg, and most likely total my bike.

But what occurred next would be far, far worse.

PARALYZED FROM THE NECK DOWN

I had never been struck by anything with such force. Frozen in an out-of-the-saddle position, both my feet were separated instantly from the pedals. My bike was ripped from under me and jettisoned away. I began to somersault and cartwheel like a rag doll, completely out of control, smashing onto the hood of the car, careening off the windshield, and then bouncing off the roof. My breath was knocked out of me, but I felt no pain—not yet.

After these violent gyrations, my body settled into a face-up position; it seemed as if I were floating to the ground. As I fell, two thoughts arose: the first one surprisingly serene. I noticed that the sky looked incredibly blue, almost artificial, as if computer-generated. I was disappointed that such a gorgeous sky and beautiful day was being wasted on such a tragic accident. To brace myself for the eventual landing, I put my hands directly above my shoulders in a palms-up position. I still was not breathing.

Then, a second thought took hold of me. Words rang out in my head I will never forget—*this is really going to hurt*!

I slammed onto Pacific Street, landing directly on my back, neck, head, and right shoulder. Then pain arrived quickly and with a vengeance. Instantly, everything reverted back to normal speed. I caught my breath. The back of my neck hurt badly, and my right shoulder felt like someone had taken a sledgehammer to it. Even worse, my right hand felt as if it were on fire.

I looked to my right to see if there were flames and was amazed not to see any. But when I turned to look at my right hand, a sharp pain emanated from my neck, just below the back of my helmet. Thankfully, the helmet had stayed on while I tumbled over the car and then landed on the road. The impact on the road was so hard, my helmet cracked in four places. I was certain at the very least, I had sustained a concussion and, at the very worst, more serious brain damage.

My knees were throbbing as I bent them toward my chest and began to rock back and forth on my back. I heard myself screaming for someone to tend to my arm and my hand, still certain my hand was engulfed in flames.

Through my haze, I saw a male driver get out of the car that just struck me, saying, "I never saw him." Then, a woman got out of the passenger side, yelling, "I never saw him either." Even in my current state, going crazy with pain and fear, I couldn't believe my ears. We were the only two moving objects on the road, and I was clearly in view. My jersey was a bright canary yellow. Adding together my height of 6'1," my helmet, and the distance my pedal was from the ground at the bottom of a revolution, I must have appeared to be a 7-foot, bright yellow, full-motion billboard. How could he not see me? What had he been doing? Why was he so distracted?

Citizen first responders were on the scene in seconds. I later learned that a man named Chris Garcia, an employee with the City of Oceanside, just happened to be sitting in his car about fifty yards ahead of the accident scene. He had started his car and was getting ready to pull away from his parallel parking space. To be certain that no traffic was approaching, he looked into his driver-side mirror and watched, in total disbelief, at the scene that was unfolding. Then, he heard a loud thud and saw me tumbling over a car that was turning left. Instinctively, he turned off his engine, jumped out, and began running north to the scene while calling 911.

Chris now stood over me, trying to assess the situation and relay the information to the 911 dispatcher. Based on the pain I was having in my right arm, in particular my pseudo-fiery right hand, he thought I had broken my arm. It was a fair assessment.

Brooke, a young woman who was visiting with friends in a house along Pacific Street, heard the same loud thud and then heard me screaming in pain. Probably seconds after Chris arrived, so did she. A mid-twenties attractive mother-to-be, Brooke had no formal medical training, yet she somehow knew to stabilize my head and neck, and I clearly let her know how badly my neck hurt. She asked me what my name was, and I found her voice utterly calming. As more people arrived at the scene, that calming voice became commanding as Brooke simply took charge. While several others came to my aid, someone suggested that removing my helmet would be a good thing. In doing so, the pain in my neck increased ten-fold. It startled me so much that I couldn't help but scream in pain. Someone shouted, "Get a towel and put it under his neck to support it." Thankfully, they did this quickly. One can only imagine what additional damage my spinal column and spinal cord might have suffered if I was not given this stabilizing support to my neck.

A motorcycle police officer arrived on the scene just moments after Chris and Brooke. I was still conscious, so he asked me if I had any ID. Through the fog of excruciating pain, I told him to call my wife, Sheri, and grunted out her cell phone number. Brooke repeated the number loudly and, in a firm voice, said, "Okay, you have a number. Call it!"

I was still moving my legs a great deal, and the pain seemed to be increasing with each movement. Paramedics had been dispatched from Oceanside Firehouse Station 2 and arrived roughly five minutes from the time I was struck. As I continued to writhe in pain, the police officer said to me, "Sir, you have to stop moving. It will only make injuries like this worse." At that precise moment, my world completely changed.

Lying on my back with my knees bent toward my chest, mysteriously, my legs slowly dropped to the ground. I became confused and temporarily forgot about the pain in my neck. Something very strange was beginning to happen to me. It felt as though a tarp, that had covered my body from just under my chin down to my toes, was being removed. Along with it, all the feeling in my body was disappearing. I tried desperately to move my feet, but there was no response. My God, what was happening to me?

I tried to lift my waist, and nothing happened. I became even more confused. This was not possible. I was almost there, at Starbucks, ready to have coffee with Sheri and, later that night, a send-off dinner with Meg and Wes. What had I done? What just happened to me? Why could I not feel anything or move anything? Why was I paralyzed from the neck down?

As Brooke continued to hold my head steady, I blurted out, "I can't feel anything below my neck! I'm scared, Brooke. What's happening to me?"

"It's okay, John," she told me, her voice gentle and reassuring. "You're going to be all right."

"Please just don't leave me," I begged. At this point in time, she represented all my hopes for survival. She was my angel.

As she continued to reassure me, my mind drifted off to a calmer, safer place. I found myself considering the two possibilities that awaited me. First, I could spend the rest of my days as a quadriplegic, similar to the fate of Christopher Reeve. I thought about how he had suffered, yet handled himself with such dignity the rest of his life and wondered if I could do the same. What impact would this have on Sheri and my children? Would I be able to cope? Did I have the courage to face what had just happened to me?

Then, my mind shifted to the second possibility—death. I was beginning to get a much better sense of the seriousness of my condition. I wondered about the extent of my internal injuries and began to think about my life—the things I had done, the things I hadn't done, and the things I was never going to be able to do.

Suddenly, a strange feeling of satisfaction began to come over me. I realized I had loved and been loved plenty, laughed often, traveled much, read extensively, golfed a great deal, ridden thousands of miles, regretted and had asked forgiveness for any transgressions, and was at peace with God. A sense of tranquility wrapped around me like a warm blanket on a cold winter's night as I came to the conclusion that if it was my time and I was going to die, it was okay.

Except that I did *not* want to die. My will to live was still strong, and although I knew my situation was extremely serious, I was far from ready to give up. Yet physically and emotionally, I was overcome with a feeling of utter and absolute helplessness. Beyond praying, there wasn't much else I could do.

You may have heard the saying, "There are no atheists in a foxhole." I can assure you that in this foxhole, there were none. While I had not formally practiced my Roman Catholic religion for over two decades, I had never lost my faith. I began saying the Hail Mary silently and repeatedly as fast as I could. It was a conditioned and natural response, and it gave me hope. If dying or paralysis were to be my fate, praying gave me the strength and courage to face the outcome.

While the firefighters/paramedics were bracing my neck and placing me on a board for transfer into the ambulance, my focus turned to Brooke. I could hear her repeating, "John, you're going to be okay. Stay with me."

It was too much to ask. The trauma my body had just sustained was too intense. I could no longer stay focused on Brooke or anything else. As her voice seemed to be drifting off into the distance, I looked up at her one last time in a futile attempt to remain conscious. Then, slowly, quietly, everything faded to black.

SURVIVING THE GOLDEN HOUR

Perhaps you've heard of the Golden Hour. This term is often used in a military context and, more broadly, for trauma patients. It refers to the span of time between the moment an injury is received to the moment a victim arrives at a Mobile Army Surgical Hospital, critical care unit, hospital trauma center, emergency room, or some other medical facility where comprehensive care can be administered. If this medical care begins within one hour of the injury, a person's chance of survival and recovery are greatly enhanced.

At 2:30 p.m. on August 21, 2009, my Golden Hour clock began to run. Ironically, at the precise moment when I was struck, my luck changed for the better. Now that the impact was behind me, things began to go my way. Chris saw me flying through the air and called 911. Brooke heard the loud thud and ran to the scene to give aid and comfort. An Oceanside police officer pulled up to the scene in just over a minute. Two firefighter/paramedic (FF/PM) units were dispatched and arrived within five minutes of the 911 call.

If I was going to be struck by a car in such a violent manner, I guess I was lucky enough to have it happen in one of the best places in the United States, and possibly the world. Not more than ten years earlier, the trauma patient mortality rate in San Diego County was 22 percent. The day of my accident, that rate was down to 2 percent. Thanks to leaders in the healthcare field, such as Chris Van Gorder, President and CEO of Scripps Health, the county had established one of the finest trauma systems anywhere.

Once on the scene, the FF/PM units quickly assessed my condition and stabilized me with a board, neck brace, and intravenous drip (IV). Captain Morhman, the ranking officer at the accident scene, quickly assessed the seriousness of the situation and whirled his right index finger skyward, giving the command to dispatch Mercy Air, the helicopter life-flight company. More good luck followed. The Mercy Air crew was available and ready to deploy on a moment's notice from their base in the Carlsbad airport. Without delay, they flew to an airfield in Oceanside, just ten miles due north, to rendezvous with the ambulance transporting me. Coincidentally, I lived less than two miles (as the helicopter flies) from Mercy Air's home base. Often I would see their life-flight helicopter either returning to base or heading for an accident scene. It never occurred to me that I might one day be in desperate need of their help.

As they put me into the ambulance, I awoke for a brief moment and realized, once again, how badly I must be injured. Then, again, I passed out. With lights flashing and sirens wailing, the ambulance whisked me from the accident scene toward the airport's tarmac about five miles away. My Golden Hour clock was ticking away precious minutes.

After they transferred me from the ambulance into the helicopter and closed the door, Buzz, a Marine Corps veteran of twenty-three years, cranked up the rotor's RPMs. With the deft touch and coolness of a battle-hardened Blackhawk pilot, he prepared to speed me along my thirty-mile life-flight to Scripps Memorial Hospital La Jolla (SMH-LJ) trauma center.

Just as the increased speed of the rotor blades sent vibrations throughout the highly compacted cabin, I awoke again, briefly. I remembered the accident. I remembered becoming paralyzed from the neck down. Also, I remembered that one of the possible outcomes was death.

To my left and my right, I could see a male flight nurse/paramedic with their flight helmets donned. Their expressions were serious as they focused on stabilizing my vital signs. Curiously, I felt no pain and still felt nothing below my neck. It was certainly an odd sensation to gaze downward along my body and see my waist and my feet, yet feel nothing. My brain told me, "Yep, they're still there," but I just couldn't feel or move them. I still had cognitive capability, which made the experience even more puzzling, but my head and my brain were now an independent part of my body, somehow detached from the rest of me.

In spite of this revelation, I felt at peace. Knowing that death was a very real possibility, I suddenly thought, *I might be going to heaven.*

Then, two other thoughts ran through my mind. First, *Wow! What a cool way this is to go to heaven! Who would have thought?* Second, *Am I being a bit too optimistic? And will I have more time here on earth to help shape the ultimate outcome?*

Unfortunately, because my injury was so severe, I lost consciousness again and cannot recall any more details of the flight.

Flying on a southern heading as fast as conditions warranted, Buzz touched down on the helipad at the SMH-LJ trauma center about twenty minutes later. As I was being wheeled on the gurney into the emergency room, I opened my eyes, which still had contact lenses on them, and saw another angel. He said, "John, I'm your nurse, Dave. I'm going to take care of you."

Somehow, judging by the tenor of his voice, I had no doubt whatsoever that he meant what he said. He proceeded to remove my contacts and to cut away my bright yellow jersey. Ironically, it was my Tour of Hope souvenir jersey I'd purchased a few years before.

Once I was safely inside the SMH-LJ emergency room, I felt a searing pain in my neck from my severely damaged spinal column. The pain was excruciating. On a pain scale of 0 to 10, the needle was pegging hard right. But I had Nurse Dave by my side, which gave me comfort, knowing that I was in excellent hands.

The clock had just struck 3:30 p.m. I was quadriplegic but still alive. My Golden Hour had run its course, and I had made it just in time!

PART II

THE SURGERIES

THE PHONE CALL

Meanwhile, at about 2:40 p.m., Sheri had received the call no one wants to get from a police officer at an accident scene. He reported I had been hit by a car and told her that it appeared I had a broken right arm. Sheri's first reaction was sadness, knowing that a broken arm would hamper my ability to ride for a while. She knew how disappointed I would be. She also knew I would be in pain and discomfort, but fortunately, it wouldn't be life-changing.

As is often the case with accidents, first reports are seldom accurate. So Sheri asked the officer if she could talk to me. When asked, I grunted to the officer, "No." This was the first time Sheri became suspicious that I might have a more severe injury.

She immediately called Meg and Wes and left them a voice mail message. She told them I had been hit by a car and probably had a broken arm and that she was headed to the accident scene in Oceanside. She would fill them in as soon as she knew more details.

Having gotten the number for police dispatch, Sheri then called to get directions to the crash site. The dispatcher helped Sheri with directions as she drove to the accident scene and reported that the ambulance had arrived, and I would be life-flighted by Mercy Air to a nearby hospital. That's when all the alarm bells went off in her head.

"What? Why is he being life-flighted for a broken arm?" Sheri asked the dispatcher incredulously.

This didn't make sense, and she began to wonder if the initial injury report was correct. She had a strong sense that things must be worse than first described, but the dispatcher, perhaps not knowing my true condition, informed Sheri that a life-flight for a cyclist who had been hit by a car was standard operating procedure— strictly a cautionary measure.

Sheri wasn't buying it. Her instincts and common sense told her otherwise, and she told the dispatcher as much. Call it her female intuition, but she knew I was hurt badly. She had to fight back the onset of panic as she continued to drive to the accident.

When she arrived at the scene, Brooke was awaiting her and told her I was on my way to Scripps Memorial Hospital La Jolla, about thirty miles south. Around this time, Meg called Sheri back. Sheri told her to get Wes and meet her in the SMH-LJ emergency room.

To this day, Sheri doesn't know how she made the thirty-mile drive. The only thing she remembers about it is listening to a Ralph Vaughn Williams piece of music, called "Fantasia on a Theme," over and over again to try to calm her nerves. She is convinced that she arrived at the emergency room safely only with the help of angels.

By the time Sheri, Meg, and Wes reconnected at the hospital, it was around 4:00 p.m., an hour and a half after I'd been struck. Emergency room personnel verified that I had indeed arrived and was in the best of hands, but still no report on my actual condition.

I had no idea my family had made it to the hospital; I was passing in and out of consciousness, totally immersed in the emergency room, trauma treatment, analysis, and diagnostic process. As soon as there was something definitive to report, Sheri had been assured that someone would brief her. She knew now, beyond any shadow of doubt, a broken arm was not the whole story. She sensed and knew to the marrow of her bones that this situation was much, much more serious.

For Sheri, Meg, and Wes, an agonizing period of waiting began, accompanied by a flood of emotions. A combination of helplessness and fear wafted over them. As tears began to well up in their eyes, they leaned into their faith, formed a circle, held hands, and began to pray.

DIAGNOSIS: QUADRIPLEGIA

When Nurse Dave wheeled me into the emergency room (ER) at 3:30 p.m., Dr. Ferkich, the attending ER physician, jumped right on the case. The Mercy Air flight crew reported to him that they had given me an IV with fentanyl, used for breakthrough pain and one hundred times more potent than morphine. Also, they indicated that my heart rate and blood pressure were dropping to dangerous levels. My desperate condition required a quick diagnosis and swift action.

After Dr. Ferkich and his team quickly stabilized my vital signs, his diagnosis identified two extremely serious conditions. First, he estimated that I had incurred a "complete" spinal cord injury at the C4 level. He described it as "complete" because I had zero sensation and no motor function from just below the neck. Second, I had gone into what is known as spinal shock. This is an ominous condition whereby, among other things, your heart is no longer receiving the proper signals to pick up its pace to elevate your heart rate and increase your blood pressure. Involuntary nerve functions cease to operate. Consequently, my heart rate slowed and my blood pressure dropped to dangerously low levels. I needed trauma team intervention, stat!

Within ten minutes, Dr. Ferkich called Dr. Tominaga, the trauma surgeon leading the trauma team response. Once their consultation was complete, Dr. Tominaga ordered a battery of tests. She instructed the attending nurse to start a large IV line and to prep a second large one, if needed. My vital signs were to be monitored every five minutes, and my EKG was to be monitored continuously, recording my heart rhythm as well as my oxygen saturation.

The doctors then inserted a Foley catheter and a Nasogastric (NG or nose) tube, a clear plastic tube through my nose, down the back of my throat, through my esophagus, and into my stomach. This allowed them to administer liquid medication on demand.

After Dr. Tominaga's secondary examination and the evidence of a complete spinal cord injury, she ordered a Neo-Synephrine drip. This improved my blood pressure, but my heart rate plummeted to the 30s. The doctors responded by starting a dopamine drip, which lifted my heart rate to the 50s. Typically, a resting heart rate is 72 bpm. As a cyclist, mine was about 45 bpm, so getting it back into the 50s was a good thing, indeed.

The next step was to initiate a Solu-Medrol spine protocol. Apparently, if this medication is administered within eight hours from the time of injury, it can provide a critical benefit by helping reduce swelling in and around the spinal cord. Additionally, I was given small doses of morphine for pain and Zofran for nausea.

The Zofran also greatly diminished another source of fear for me. Because I was unable to move, I had been afraid of becoming nauseous and choking on my own vomit. Once the Zofran kicked in, the nausea dissipated and my fear of choking dissolved. It was now 4:00 p.m., amazingly only ninety minutes from when I was struck by the car.

Dr. Tominaga then ordered a chest X-ray and a CT (computed tomography) scan of my head/neck/chest/abdomen/pelvis to look for breaks and other possible damage, an MRI (magnetic resonance imaging) of the cervical spine to identify soft tissue damage to any disc and the spinal cord, and an MRA (magnetic resonance angiogram) to determine the extent of any blood vessel damage. After reviewing the imaging results with two radiologists, it was abundantly clear to Dr. Tominaga that my injuries were serious and life-threatening. This is how she documented her findings:

1. New onset quadriplegia with acute spinal cord injury with large extruded C5-C6 disc herniation

2. Neurogenic (spinal) shock

3. Right vertebral artery injury

4. Right C6 lateral mass and facet fracture

5. C6 vertebral body fracture

6. C6 foramen transverse fracture

7. Facial abrasions with laceration

8. Bilateral knee abrasions with left knee contusions

9. Left forearm abrasion

As if the spinal cord injury weren't enough, #3 on my hit parade was also quite serious. Because of the life-threatening damage to my right vertebral artery, Dr. Sedwitz, the director of vascular surgery, was consulted. A course of action needed to be decided—perform surgery to eliminate the possibility of a blood clot releasing from the damaged artery and traveling to my brain, which could cause a massive stroke or death, or perform spine surgery. Dr. Sedwitz recommended proceeding with a spine stabilization surgery first. Further vertebral artery injury evaluation would be performed after the spine surgery and would involve a neuro-interventional radiologist.

Ironically, only six months earlier, Scripps had recruited doctors with this exact and rare specialty. This, too, would prove to be another stroke (or prevention of one) of luck for me.

By now, it was 5:00 p.m., and enough was known about my situation for Dr. Tominaga to meet with my family. She found them in the waiting room and invited them into a smaller, more private anteroom. Sheri will never forget that heart-stopping meeting.

> When Meg, Wes, and I were invited into the small consultation office just off the emergency room, we were certainly not prepared for what we heard from Dr. Tominaga.

"John's had a severe spinal cord injury," was how she started matter-of-factly. "He is in very serious condition and we are continuing to run tests. I can tell you that we have completed the MRI scan of his head, and at least there's no brain damage."

"When can we see him?" I asked.

"Not yet. We need to finish our scan evaluations first and then consult a neurosurgeon."

Dr. Tominaga's words made me feel like I had been kicked in the gut. My world was crashing around me. I had suspected John's injury was worse than a broken arm, but I could never have imagined something this severe or this frightening. For the second time in as many hours, the color had gone out of my face, just as it had when I received the call from the officer at the accident scene. I tried to grasp the magnitude of what the doctor was saying, but it just made no sense. How could this be? Had I not been sitting, I'm certain I would have fainted.

Frankly, while there was much Dr. Tominaga said, there was much she didn't say. My mind raced as I tried to fill in the blanks and piece together the events of the last few hours. I dared a glimpse into the future; what I saw shook me to my core.

As the doctor left us on her way back to John's trauma center room, I turned to Meg and Wes. They, too, seemed in shock and disbelief. We looked at one another as if we were ghosts. Instinctively, we joined hands, fought back the tears, and began to pray, again.

Now, it was time for Dr. Tominaga to consult with Dr. Leary, the attending neurosurgeon. This mild-mannered, highly trained, and intensely focused thirty-seven-year-old neurosurgeon brought experience and insight to my case beyond his years of clinical practice. Dr. Tominaga met him in surgery and showed him my MRI images and said with a sense of urgency, "We have a quad here, and he's in spinal shock. What do you think?"

He quickly arrived at his conclusion and told her with a heightened sense of urgency, "I need to operate on him as soon as I am finished with this surgery. I will examine him myself once I am finished here."

After he completed his examination of me, Dr. Leary was further convinced that emergency surgery was my best and only hope. Given all the conditions I was presenting, other surgeons may have waited several days for the swelling around my spinal injury to decrease. Had he chosen that course of action, the results would have been very different. My fate to live the rest of my days in a wheelchair as a quadriplegic would have been sealed.

It was now about 5:30 p.m. During the last three hours, I had run the gamut of activity. I had started out safely enjoying a short and easy afternoon ride, which ended tragically. I'd been comforted by citizen responders, stabilized by firefighters and paramedics with a neck brace and back board, transported via ambulance then life-flighted thirty miles, seamlessly passed from the emergency room staff to the trauma team, administered the proper drug protocols to keep me alive and to control swelling/heart rate/blood pressure, examined with every imaging technology available, and fast-tracked on a path to the operating room.

It would be up to Dr. Leary to do what all the years of his training and clinical practice had prepared him to do. He had operated on hundreds of other patients with similar injuries and knew my chances for even the slightest recovery, such as moving my fingers, was less than 1 percent. The summation of his experience brought him to a singular conclusion—even with surgery, I would likely be wheelchair bound and probably quadriplegic. But even that 1 percent chance to perhaps move some fingers required immediate surgery, and for that, he needed Sheri's consent and mine.

THE CONSULTATION AT THE GURNEY

By 6:00 p.m., Sheri was still reeling from the initial shock from the meeting with Dr. Tominaga. It takes more than one hour to come to grips with being told your husband is now completely paralyzed from just below the neck. But there was no time to waste. Dr. Leary knew time was of the essence. He asked Nurse Dave to get Sheri and bring her to the trauma room where I was. He needed to show her the extent and seriousness of my injury in the hope of getting permission to proceed with surgery. I recall very little about the period of time from when I arrived at SMH-LJ on the helipad to this point. Yet I remember this examination and consultation as though it happened one hour ago.

This was the first time Sheri met Dr. Leary and the first time she had seen me since I left our home for my ride. I looked quite different, with a large gash above my left eye, bruises and cuts on my knees, a stabilizing neck brace, and multiple IVs. In addition, I was struggling to cope with extreme pain emanating from my neck. Most shocking for her was seeing me lying on my back, completely motionless. The scene was almost more than she could take. She became light-headed as she tried to focus on Dr. Leary's words.

The doctor knew the clock was ticking, so he immediately got down to business. As I lay face up on the gurney covered with a blanket, he began to describe my injuries to Sheri as "severe and life-threatening." After removing the blanket covering me, he showed Sheri a marker line across my chest drawn above the nipples. He indicated from that point down, I was completely paralyzed—no sensation and no motor function whatsoever.

That was all it took to put Sheri over the top, both physically and emotionally. She began to feel faint and asked for a chair. Nurse Dave was right there to help her.

Once Sheri steadied herself, Dr. Leary proceeded to show her evidence of my paralysis. He asked me to reply yes if I could feel him poking me in various places below the marker line. Each time, I responded helplessly, "No."

At that moment, I saw the fear washing over Sheri. I knew she was trying hard not to show it, but when you're as close to someone as I am to her, there simply was no way for her to hide it. Once again, I thought of Christopher Reeve and our future.

Dr. Leary then demonstrated to Sheri that I had a complete absence of feeling in the rectum and was in spinal shock—both ominous indicators of how badly I was injured. He knew he had to operate immediately if I were to have any chance of even the slightest recovery. I remember him being quite clear about the risks and that he could not guarantee any specific results. Then, he told us that even if we allowed him to operate, then and there, he gave me "less than 1 percent chance of any recovery." He suggested that I might be able to move some fingers or perhaps my shoulders. He gave no mention or even a hint of me walking again someday. Dr. Leary's assessment of my condition, his diagnosis and prognosis, while delivered honestly and compassionately, was almost beyond our comprehension.

That was the first moment when it truly sunk in—I was going to live the rest of my life in a wheelchair. I was scared, confused, and in total disbelief. As I gazed into Sheri's eyes, I could tell she was as frightened as me. I felt so sorry for what I had just done to burden her for the rest of her life. Even though the accident was not my fault, I felt enormous amounts of guilt and helplessness. I wanted desperately to reach out and hold her, kiss her. Nothing would move.

Faced with my complicated and serious condition, Dr. Leary implored us to give him the permission to proceed with surgery, immediately. At the same time, he informed us that many renowned hospitals might follow a different protocol and wait several days before operating and allow the swelling to dissipate. His best medical advice, however, was that we *not* wait another moment.

By now, Sheri had recovered somewhat from this all too surreal scene and from trying to comprehend the events of the last three-plus hours. Her response to Dr. Leary was measured and firm.

"John and I make these types of big decisions as a team. As for me, I say yes, operate." Then, she looked down at me and asked, "John, what do you want to do?"

"Sheri, please let him operate right away. I think it's my only chance."

Without saying it, she and I both knew what that "chance" represented. It meant turning the clock backward to before 2:30 p.m. and regaining at least part of the life we'd had as an inseparable couple. Maybe I would only be able to move some fingers or a hand or my shoulders. Moving something would be better than moving nothing. I didn't care if it was only a 1 percent chance. Not operating meant a 0 percent chance! We both agreed to proceed.

As soon as Sheri signed the consent form for the surgery, Dr. Leary's surgical team moved into action swiftly. It was about 6:30 p.m. I remember Sheri giving me a kiss and telling me things were going to be okay. Within minutes, Meg and Wes appeared briefly to give me their love and encouragement and to say they were praying for me.

Then, what seemed like another angel appeared to me. As he wheeled me toward the operating room, he introduced himself and said he would be part of Dr. Leary's surgical team. I remember him saying to me, "John, I'm Dr. Pettit. I'm your anesthesiologist. We're going to take care of you."

For the next few minutes, I wondered what was to become of me. Things seemed to be happening so quickly, and while I was comforted and encouraged by Dr. Pettit's words, I had no idea what awaited me on the other side of surgery. Would I live? Would I still be quadriplegic? How much would I recover, if any? What would I be able to do for myself? What would life in a wheelchair be like? What had I done to Sheri's life? How much of a burden would I be to her? Why did this happen to me? I kept thinking how insane and unreal all of this was. It must be a nightmare. Someone, anyone, please wake me!

Once in the surgical suite, I sensed a number of people donned in surgical gowns and masks moving about quickly, but deliberately, prepping for my operation. I knew that my life and my future would be impacted by how well they performed. I began to do the only thing I could think of doing—continuously reciting the Hail Mary to myself.

At 6:46 p.m., the anesthesia IV drip began. My future now clearly rested in the hands of Dr. Leary, his surgical team, and God.

LIKE NO OTHER SURGERY I'D PERFORMED

The operating theater was prepared and John was rushed in. He required two IV drips just to maintain his blood pressure. A powerful steroid was being administered to try to counteract swelling in the spinal cord. I opened the anterior part of his neck and dissected down to the front of the spine. The anterior ligament between C5 and C6 was torn and there was a fracture of the C6 bone. There was a huge hole in the C5-6 intervertebral disc, as if someone had bored it out with a large corkscrew. Using a high-powered operating microscope, I carefully removed that part of the disc and inspected the area behind the vertebral bodies. The posterior ligament was shredded and had been stripped from the adjoining bone edges. Under the ligament was an enormous fragment of disc that was crushing the spinal cord. Using small hooks, I extracted the disc fragment and widely decompressed the spinal cord. I further inspected the spinal cord, and amazingly, it began to pulse normally.

A feeling came over me at that exact moment that is difficult to explain. All my years of training, study, and research told me that John's injury was permanent and that he had no chance of a meaningful recovery. But I wanted to believe it could happen. I'd performed this particular procedure hundreds of times before, but something about this case felt different. I looked up from the operating table and glanced at the clock. It was 8:20 p.m., just under six hours from impact. At that moment, I announced to my team in the room, "We could be miracle workers tonight!"

I completed the operation by replacing the herniated disc with a cage packed with bone graft. The bones and fractures were stabilized with a titanium plate and screws fusing C5 to C6. The surgery took a little more than an hour to perform, but it was the most important hour in John's life to date.

John went to the surgical ICU for his post-operative care. It was essential for him to display signs of neurologic recovery in the next twenty-four hours. He needed to move something, anything, a finger, a toe. The persistence of a complete spinal cord injury beyond twenty-four hours confirms that no additional function will return.

What happened next exceeded my wildest expectations. I was witness to a miracle.

IT WENT WELL—NOW WE WAIT

The first person who spoke to Sheri, Meg, and Wes after the surgery was Dr. Pettit.

"The surgery went well," he said encouragingly. Knowing the surgery could have gone differently, the three of them finally got a moment of relief. Still, Sheri was anxious to speak directly with Dr. Leary. What he had to say would carry a great deal of weight.

Within a few minutes, Dr. Leary appeared before the family. He had cautious, but encouraging news to report. "It went well, but now we have to wait."

"What will success look like?" Sheri asked.

Without hesitation, Dr. Leary replied, "We need to see John move something, anything, within the next twelve to twenty-four hours. If he does, it will be a very good sign."

"And if he doesn't move something?"

"Most likely, John will be quadriplegic and in a wheelchair the rest of his life."

Hearing those words was one thing. Comprehending them was altogether a different matter. For Sheri, Meg, and Wes, another emotionally charged waiting period had just begun. It was time for them to give other family members and relatives the latest update.

Sheri called her mom to let her know my status. Meg called her brother, Matt, to bring him up to speed. Wes informed his family. All three of them were asking for prayers. During the next several days, Sheri would contact more friends and family to share the latest news, and many had already begun to pray for my recovery. A confluence of science and faith was well underway, all on my behalf.

While Dr. Leary had been briefing my family, hospital staff transferred me from the operating room to Room 12 in the Surgical Intensive Care Unit (SICU). Then, the impressive SICU team began their detailed work to assure I received optimum care.

Their immediate tasks included monitoring my vital signs, checking for any bleeding, assessing the drain from the surgical incision, watching my color, measuring my temperature, securing all monitors, and administering proper fluids and medications through my five IVs. The team carefully observed my awakening from anesthesia to watch for complications and manage my pain level appropriately.

As I gradually came out of my surgical stupor and the influence of the anesthesia, I gazed to my left and saw Nurse Brian tending to my multiple IV drips. He had a peaceful and calming smile on his face. The comfort it gave lasted only moments. Each passing minute brought me further into a conscious and incredibly strange new world. IV drips hung next to me like floating water balloons. Monitors seemed to be everywhere, softly beeping with their digital readouts. I could barely swivel my head from side to side to scan the dimly lit room. Something seemed to be in my mouth and throat. I thought I was choking. I wanted to reach up and get it out, but my arms would not respond.

My God, I remembered. I was paralyzed. I could not move my waist, arms, hands, fingers, feet, or toes. Except for my head, I couldn't move a thing. Yes, I was alive, but I was extremely confused and afraid.

After what seemed like an eternity to us all, it was time for my family to see me. Before entering Room 12, Nurse Brian informed them that I was stable, gave them an update on my condition, counseled them on what they were about see, and brought them in at about 10:00 p.m.

I remember seeing Sheri first. She reached out and stroked my hair. Instinctively, she knew I needed to feel her touch, and my head was one place she knew I would. I became emotionally overwhelmed. Even though the ET tube prevented me from speaking, Sheri knew what I was trying to say. As she looked into my eyes, she read my thoughts—I loved her with my whole heart, and I was utterly confused and frightened.

Then I saw Meg and Wes. As Wes stood by, Sheri and Meg were smiling and continued to touch my head. They tried to tell me what had happened and that I had just come out of spine surgery. Although my brain was still in somewhat of a fog from the remnants of the anesthesia, I knew something was terribly wrong. What in the world was I doing in this large hospital room surrounded with hanging tubes, floating bags of fluid, and high-tech monitors? The entire scene seemed like a continuation of a very bad nightmare. Why wouldn't someone just wake me up and make it go away?

As Sheri's voice began to penetrate my consciousness, my thinking came to a screeching halt. She could tell my thoughts had just gone to a dark place and could see the terror begin to well up inside of me. My anxiety and fear were getting out of control.

As only she could, Sheri began to tell me calmly what had happened and that I had just been operated on by Dr. Leary. She told me that we had reason to be hopeful. Still in a fog from the surgery and pain medication, I let her words comfort me like a warm shower after a long, arduous ride. I was beginning to realize the gravity of my situation and how completely dependent I was on the care and professionalism of the hospital staff.

Now past 11:00 p.m. and well past the "official" visiting hours, the SICU team told Sheri, Meg, and Wes that they needed to leave so I could rest. Just before they did, Sheri kissed me on the forehead and tried to answer the question she knew was foremost in my mind: "What happens now?"

"The next twelve to twenty-four hours are very important, John," she told me. "The nurses will be looking for any sign of movement—anything at all."

Her statement was short and to the point, which is all I could process anyway, and she knew it. How she seemed so resolute and hopeful was beyond me. She told me later that as fearful as she, Meg, and Wes were, they were determined to never let me see it. They would stay in faith, continue to pray, and only believe in a positive outcome.

As they walked out of Room 12 after saying good-bye, I noticed I could read the time on the wall clock fifteen feet away. I found that rather odd since I was nearsighted and without the benefit of glasses or contact lenses. A small consolation prize, I thought, for what had just happened to me. I also thought about what Sheri had told me. It resonated deeply. I knew I had to move something, anything.

Then, in the most unobtrusive way, Nurse Brian did his usual IV inspections, took my vital sign measurements, and completed his hourly neurological exam. To help me with the high level of pain, he administered some morphine. It felt like ice going down my left side and back up my right.

Wait! Had I just felt something? Lying motionless and intubated prevented me from reacting to this very strange sensation.

Before I could give it another thought, the morphine did its magic and eliminated my pain. I closed my eyes and drifted off to a more peaceful, restful place.

A MORNING OF FIRSTS

Dr. Leary estimates it was just over thirty minutes from the beginning of surgery when he removed my massively ruptured and herniated disc. At that moment, my spinal cord was no longer compressed, marking the point in time when I was given a chance to begin to heal and to recover, although no one knew if or how much I would.

It may have been far less than a one-in-a-million chance, but at least I had it. My body had gone through an incredible experience during the first six hours after the accident. It was a good thing I was now in the care of the SICU staff.

There's a reason why the word *intensive* is included in the name, Surgical Intensive Care Unit. Round-the-clock monitoring, testing, medication administration, patient positioning, IV and catheter maintenance, and many other vital observations and reporting are done by doctors, nurses, and other SICU staff. All of this activity and patient progress is meticulously tracked every hour of every day. My spinal cord injury required that an extensive neurological exam record be updated hourly.

In my case, some items were checked and documented every fifteen minutes. A critical care flowsheet was used to document a variety of data, including vital signs, pain, sedation, drips, fluid intake and output, and much more. Both of these documentation tools helped the SICU staff and physicians to precisely monitor my status and progress and to seamlessly hand off my care from one shift to the other.

I remember waking up around midnight. I was in a state of total disbelief and wished with all my might that I would wake from this nightmare. My family had left for the night, the light in the room was down, and Nurse Brian was at my bedside. He was tending to my Foley catheter output and various boluses for the IVs. Because it was the top of the hour, he began working through his checklist on both the critical care flowsheet and the neurological exam record. I was still under the influence of a sedative, painkillers, and a whole gamut of medications.

Even through the fog of these, I began to comprehend the events of yesterday. I had been in a very bad accident, had undergone major surgery, and was now in intensive care. Unfortunately, I realized it wasn't a dream. While my mind seemed to be in a state of shock, I was certain of one thing: I'm still alive!

Then, as a feeling of helplessness had begun to grip me, I found myself buoyed by Nurse Brian's positive bedside manner. In fact, he was so positive, it was infectious. His constant smile and the way he spoke to me made me think that I wasn't in that bad of shape. Of course, nothing could have been further from the truth.

Throughout the early morning hours of Saturday, I continued to fall in and out of sleep for very short periods. Each time I awoke, I understood my predicament a little bit more. During this time, Nurse Brian continued his periodic exams, prompting me for answers as to my ability to feel and move. Being intubated prevented me from giving him verbal responses. I was only able to respond by nodding my head with an answer to his yes-or-no questions. Unfortunately, my answer was always no.

Obviously, the reason for my intubation was to maintain proper function of my respiratory system. It's always better to be breathing than not. At the same time, however, it made me feel like I was choking and gasping for air, which petrified me. Consequently, the tube's presence motivated me to get the irritating medical apparatus out of my throat and mouth as soon as possible. If I had had the use of my arms and been able to reach it, I would have yanked the tube out in a flash. As it was, my tongue got quite the workout trying to expel the contraption, but to no avail.

I needed to dwell on something else besides self-extraction of this frustrating breathing device. I remembered Sheri telling me how important it was that I moved something as soon as I could. It wasn't completely clear to me just then how significant any movement might be, but if Sheri said it was important, I needed to try. I remember around 6:30 a.m. saying to myself, "Let's see if I can move my waist slightly off the bed."

The two last times I had tried were at the accident scene while lying on the road and then while inside the Mercy Air helicopter. Both of those attempts were unsuccessful. It was time to try it again.

To my utter amazement, I could do it! Just to be sure, I tried it again. Yes, my waist had definitely lifted up! Not much, but it did move.

Next, I thought, *Well, if that worked, let's try wiggling some fingers.* My right hand was still in a ball and completely numb, but my left hand was ready to try. I gave it a go, and I did it. I actually wiggled some fingers. I wasn't sure which ones, but by God, I'd done it!

Lastly, I looked down at my feet as they rested on their heels. "Could I rock those puppies back and forth and maybe wiggle some toes?" I asked myself. You bet your sweet IV I could! At that moment, I had no idea how much I would recover or what my "new normal" would look like. What I knew was this: I had sensation and movement, both of which I thought I might never have again.

I became filled with wonderment and inspiration. I screamed inside my head, "Hey! I'm not paralyzed!" I wanted desperately to tell someone. Emotionally and spiritually shaken by the thought that God may have worked a miracle, I resolved to do whatever I needed to do to recover as far as he wanted me to go.

Finally, the time came for Nurse Brian to complete his 7:00 a.m. neurological exam. Progressing with his checklists one last time before his shift ended, he probed to see if I had any sensation in both my upper extremities. Eureka! To his amazement and mine, I felt something and responded by nodding yes. Taken aback, he checked to see if I had sensation in my trunk. Again, I nodded yes. Even under sedation, I know my eyes got pretty big. He soon discovered my ability to slightly move my left fingers, rock my feet, and wiggle some toes.

Immediately after finishing his exam at about 7:30 a.m., he made a dash to the phone and called Sheri. He had promised the night before that he would call her with any significant updates. Without holding back any enthusiasm, Nurse Brian told her I had moved fingers and toes and could feel him poking my arms and legs. He said this was a very good first sign of recovery. Sheri, who usually is in control of her emotions, burst into tears and thanked him for sharing the fantastic news.

Light-years separated the message of this phone call from the one she had received from the police officer at the accident scene just seventeen hours prior. Unlike that one, Nurse Brian's call vanquished some of her fear and filled her with immeasurable hope.

YOU'RE MY MIRACLE BOY

At 8:00 a.m., Dr. Leary called the SICU to get an update from the morning duty nurse. He was eager to hear of any signs of improved sensation or movement. What he heard that morning blew him away and made his day. As soon as he learned that I had some feeling and movement, he knew I had a chance for some recovery, although to what extent was still unknown.

Dr. Tominaga received a similar update at about 9:30 a.m. She, too, was encouraged. However, both doctors knew I was in the very early stages of recovery, which tempered their reactions. Also, I remained in grave danger from the severely damaged right vertebral artery. If a blood clot should form, release, and travel to my brain, it would cause a massive stroke or, worse, death. I was hardly out of the woods.

Despite my ongoing intensive care and the potentially life-threatening condition of my damaged artery, we all celebrated that morning. Around 11:30 a.m., Dr. Leary came to my bedside for my first post-op examination. By now, my alertness level had increased and I was responding immediately to commands. As he approached my bedside, I remember seeing something on his face that had been absent when I saw him the night before, prior to surgery.

Today, he was wearing a huge grin.

He reintroduced himself as the neurosurgeon from last night, and I nodded that I remembered him. He proceeded to explain the surgery he had performed. I had a thousand questions I wanted to ask, but my ET tube kept me quiet.

Then, he started his neurological exam. As he checked to see if I had sensation in places all over my body, I was able to respond with an affirmative nod. Then he asked me if I could wiggle some fingers in my left hand (my right hand was still reasonably numb, unresponsive, and closed like a fist). To his total delight and mine, I wiggled away. He then moved his attention to my feet and asked me if I could rock them back and forth on my heels. Again, I showed him I could.

Finally, he asked me if I could wiggle some toes. I was able to move some in both feet, even better than a few hours ago. Instantly, Dr. Leary began grinning from ear to ear and exclaimed, "John, you are my miracle boy!"

To my delight, he ordered the removal of my endotrachial tube. Also, he ordered the drugs that controlled the swelling to be discontinued in twenty-four hours. The process of getting off all the medications, mineral supplements, and various chemical agents had begun. Even though it was a small step in the right direction, I felt a tinge of victory.

Last, he ordered a follow-up MRI of my cervical spine and brain. He wanted to know how the fusion of my C5 and C6 looked and to be certain that there was, indeed, no brain damage. Better safe than sorry.

I was disappointed to learn that Dr. Tominaga wasn't so sure about removing the ET tube. She wanted to review the results of the MRI later that day and be certain that I could breathe without assistance. I wish I could have weighed in on her discussion with Dr. Leary, but the doctors knew best and agreed to wait until the afternoon for extubation, once the MRI results were known.

Dr. Pettit, the anesthesiologist during my surgery, came by to say hello and to see how I was doing. He had heard that I'd moved something and wanted to see what it was. He knew how I had been injured and was particularly empathetic, given that he, too, was a cyclist. After watching me move what I could and testing me for sensation in various places, he looked at me and declared, "John, you are going to recover 100 percent."

I couldn't have heard more encouraging words that morning. Just a few minutes before, I was elated to know that the ET tube was going bye-bye and I was getting off one powerful drug. Next, Dr. Pettit was telling me that I would have a full recovery. Given my present condition, I wasn't at all sure what the path to a full recovery would look like. But if Dr. Pettit thought I could achieve it, then so would I.

Soon after Dr. Pettit left, Sheri and Meg were allowed into Room 12. Frankly, I cannot imagine what it must be like for patients in the SICU without the kind of daily family support I received. By its very name, being in the SICU implies that you are in need of some high tech, round-the-clock, professional care. It may also be fair to assume that your world was turned upside down, as was mine.

Having Sheri, Meg, and Wes there for me meant so much. Resting on my back with my head at a thirty-degree angle with tubes and IVs aplenty, I felt quite helpless. My family's presence made all the difference. They became my umbilical cord to normalcy. When Sheri and Meg were at my bedside, they made a point to keep constant contact with me by rubbing my hair, touching my shoulders, and holding my hands (even though the right one had yet to awaken).

Their visits quickly came to hold a great deal of importance to me. Consequently, I remember becoming significantly agitated one morning when they were let into my room about twenty minutes later than usual. Although the reason was perfectly legitimate, I did not want to be denied a single minute with them. How lucky for me that they were so dedicated to be there every day for ten hours? A tip-of-the-hat goes to Wes who dutifully remained in the waiting room, ran errands, and got food for the family on most days to allow Sheri and Meg visiting time since the SICU strictly followed a two-visitors-at-a-time protocol.

At around 2:00 p.m., I was rolled out of the SICU and taken for the follow-up MRI of the brain and cervical spine. By 4:00 p.m., I was back in Room 12. The key findings included confirmation of proper placement of the PEEK cage (an artificial vertebral spacer), stable titanium plate and screws, normal brain function, and the damaged right vertebral artery. To my delight, Dr. Tominaga gave the order to begin weaning me off the ET tube. By 7:00 p.m., it was out. Hallelujah!Sheri and Meg were there when I was freed from my tube and able, once again, to speak. It was wonderful to be able to talk again, if only at a whisper with a raspy voice. My arms, which had regained some mobility and had been strapped down to keep me from yanking out the ET tube, were set free. Wicked sore throat or not, it was great to be back to the land of the talking.

In fact, once the extubation was completed, I immediately recalled that famous quote from Dr. Martin Luther King Jr. (with a slight modification): "Free at last…free at last…Thank God Almighty, I'm free at last!"

Late in the day, Dr. Tominaga had begun to brief me and Sheri on another vital operation I needed. This one would address the damage to my right vertebral artery. She made no bones about the seriousness of my condition and the potential risks the damaged artery posed and had discussed the situation earlier with Dr. Leary and Dr. Sedwitz. Both concurred that the operation should be done as soon as possible—on Sunday afternoon, August 23.

Notwithstanding the danger my damaged artery presented, the thought of another operation took the wind out of my sails. I didn't know it at the time, but Sheri admitted later that the thought of an additional operation made her very nervous. She just wouldn't let me hear anything but positive words and reinforcement from her, though.

Fortunately, Drs. Barr and Ammirati, who had come to Scripps recently to establish a leading-edge neurovascular interventional practice, were brought into my case. Coincidentally, Dr. Leary had helped to recruit them to Scripps, and tomorrow, I would meet them both in surgery.

For the rest of the evening, my neurological exam results continued to improve. I was gaining more strength and more sensation by the hour. Also, I was being weaned off three more medicines, which was more cause for celebration.

Nurse Brian was back on his night shift with his usual positive demeanor, giving Sheri and Meg updates and support. Relieved, the women told me to sleep well and then headed home for some well-deserved rest. As for me, I began watching the clock, hoping to speed its pace and hasten their return.

By late evening, the pain in my neck, throat, and shoulder was getting the better of me. As Nurse Brian administered morphine, I could feel it coursing through my body—down one side and up the other. The speed with which the pain dissolved made me understand how people can become addicted to narcotics so quickly. I had seen firsthand what drugs could do to people I had known. I was determined not to be one of its victims.

Before drifting off, I began wondering about tomorrow's surgery. I figured the aftereffects of the vascular surgery could not possibly be as dramatic as the spine surgery. Then again, I wasn't clear what the surgery entailed or how delicate or dangerous the procedure would be. I had no more energy left to think about it. Instead, I chose to dwell on the amazing event of the day—I had moved and felt something! This was incredibly uplifting and a sign of much better things to come.

Trying to keep tomorrow's surgery out of my mind, I closed my eyes and began to pray. Lulled by the rhythmic beeps of the monitors, I surrendered to an incredibly deep and peaceful sleep.

THE TACKLING IS DONE— NOW WE DO THE BLOCKING

After my morning chest X-ray indicating all was well, Nurse Brian was relieved by my day-shift nurse Erin, who had been assigned to me since my arrival in Room 12. Like all the professionals involved with my case, Nurse Erin was equally terrific. Other nurses, including Jeremiah and Rachel, were just as stellar. When nurses give you the sense that you are the only patient on the planet, you know they were born with the caring gene.

I cannot overstate how powerful the feeling of being cared for was for my recovery. As a patient in the Surgical Intensive Care Unit, my ability to function and perform the slightest task had been reduced to practically zero. Just like a newborn, my very existence depended on the actions of those around me. My doctors, nurses, technicians, and specialists knew full well their responsibilities to keep me and my fellow patients alive and on the road to healing. What I witnessed at the hospital was a professional, cheerful, and compassionate team doing its level best to help all of us through our times of desperate need.

Once Sheri and Meg arrived around 10:30 a.m., things got really interesting. Dr. Leary and Dr. Barr each paid a visit to my bedside to let us know what they had in mind. The area needing intervention was my right vertebral artery opposite the C6 vertebra. In the accident, it had been severely damaged and twisted like a pretzel, creating the potential for a blood clot releasing to my brain and causing a massive stroke or death. The surgery, which was minimally invasive, would prevent this from happening.

After we heard the description of the procedure and considered the risks of not performing the surgery, Sheri and I quickly gave our consent. The operation was scheduled to begin at 4:00 p.m. and would take me out of the SICU for about two hours. It sounded pretty straightforward, although I was probably too medicated to care. On the other hand, Sheri was taking nothing for granted. She understood the unique expertise the doctors possessed, but she also knew that every surgery came with its own set of risks. While optimistic, she was still concerned about the outcome.

After Dr. Barr left my room, Dr. Leary remained at my bedside. He told Sheri and me that he was going to have to perform a second cervical spine surgery, posterior, to repair the fractured C6 vertebra. He planned to operate on Tuesday, two days from today. I'd be lightly sedated, the procedure would not take long, and there would be no post-op pain. Best of all, any risk of this surgery causing a blood clot to the brain by disturbing my damaged artery would have been eliminated by the vertebral artery embolization.

On the other hand, having another surgery on my cervical spine, where I'd been operated on two days earlier, seemed like an entirely different proposition from the embolization. The embolization would use a catheter to navigate through my vascular system to deposit some platinum coils to block blood flow. Posterior surgery on my spine would be more invasive. Since all we had to compare it to was my Friday night spine surgery, we were easily distressed. Dr. Leary did his best to explain why the second spine surgery was necessary, but it didn't help us much. We felt like we'd been kicked in the gut.

Luckily, we were given something else for us to focus on instead of that afternoon's vascular surgery and a possible second spine surgery two days later—learning how to swallow. It was time for my first swallow test. Bree, the speech pathologist, had brought in a wonderful repast of pureed food (I think it was a pumpkin concoction) and something that passed as a thick liquid. Moving my esophagus aside to expose my spine and remove my ruptured disc, and then hosting the ET tube for what seemed like an eternity, had left my throat pretty sore. Since anything liquid was being fed to me through my NG tube, I hadn't noticed just how sore it was until then.

Once Bree began testing my tolerance for the puree delight and thick liquid, I realized these foods were all I could handle. Because my arms and hands were still far from fully functional, I had to be fed by spoon. Being able to swallow even some of the pureed food, however, felt like I had achieved another big milestone. In my condition, baby steps looked huge.

As planned, Dr. Newlin, the anesthesiologist, came to Room 12 about 3:15 p.m. to go over her role in the forthcoming operation to embolize my artery. This time, Sheri and I gave our signed consent with mine being nothing more than some feeble mark I made using my left hand. Then I was transported by gurney to Angiographic Suite #17, where I arrived around 4:05 p.m., right on schedule.

The light sedation began to work its magic. I distinctly remember seeing what seemed like a room full of people and wondered why so many people were needed for a surgery that was supposed to be straightforward. Fortunately, this highly delicate and intricate operation had no complications. Things went so well, the surgeons took some extra time to examine other vessels in the immediate area. They wanted to be certain nothing had been missed in a previous MRA. When they finished, it was "two thumbs up" and "all clear."

Before the operation, Sheri had seen Drs. Barr and Ammirati in the hallway. The latter wore a particularly large grin. Sheri commented that she hoped to see the same wide grin after the surgery was completed—on both their faces. To her great delight, when she saw them two hours later, they both were sporting big grins. By 6:00 p.m. on Sunday evening, I was back in Room 12 and looking forward to throwing back some gourmet puree with a thick liquid chaser with a little help from Sheri or Meg.

Later that evening, Sheri sent an e-mail to two friends of mine, Mike and Fred. She wanted to let them know what had happened to me and my current status. I had met Mike while we were both members of a golf club in southern California. Ironically, Mike was the one who had encouraged me to take up cycling and helped me to choose my road bike. I purchased it, almost to the day, five years before the accident.

Fred was a high school buddy and was the starting center of our varsity basketball team. I was the starting point guard. We had reconnected the year before my accident after thirty-six years of life taking us in different directions. When we struck up our friendship again, it seemed as though we had not skipped a beat.

Fred and I were connected on another level, as well. On August 22, 1971, two weeks before the beginning of our senior year, we lost a friend and fellow teammate, Tom Kiley, to a tragic waterskiing accident. When Sheri first notified Fred of my accident, the first thought that entered his mind was, "Oh no—not John on almost the same day?" His e-mail response to Sheri said it all:

> Hi Sheri,
>
> Shocking news, but thanks for the info/update. I really don't know what to say other than our thoughts are with you both.
>
> What you describe sounds truly miraculous—that he can move all the important parts is fantastic and very encouraging. Yes, it will be a long road ahead, but the John that I know from so many years ago is goal-oriented,

disciplined, and determined (as I am sure that you know), so I am certain he will succeed.

Please keep me up on how things are going, and please call on me if there is anything I can do. With e-mail, the Internet, phones, and planes, the continent is not that big anymore.

I am just speechless.

Please give John my best, and my best to you.

Fred

With friends like Mike and Fred rooting for me, as well as my family, with the help of God's grace I would continue to draw strength from their outpouring of love, prayers, and encouragement.

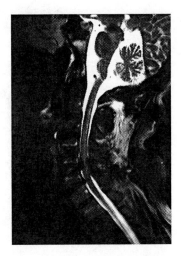

MRI scan showing a massive disc herniation compressing the spinal cord

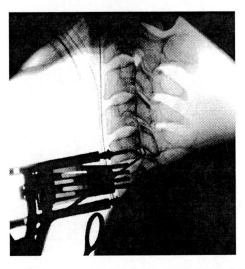

Intraoperative image showing a hook behind the C5 vertebral body to extract the ruptured disc fragment

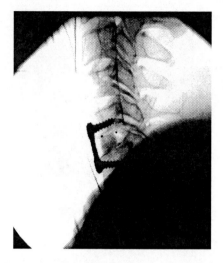

Intraoperative image showing the fusion with titanium plate and screws

Immediate post-op MRI showing completely decompressed spinal cord with a contusion (bruise) inside the spinal cord

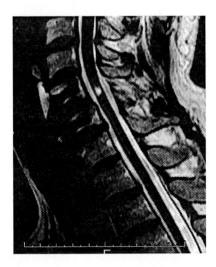

MRI at one year post-op showing a small residual area (white spot) of dead spinal cord

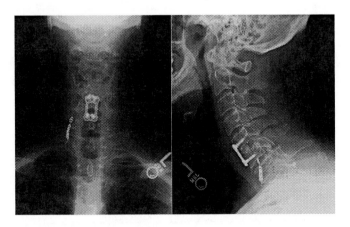

Final X-ray images of the fusion. Also note the coils inside the right vertebral artery

FACING A SECOND SPINE SURGERY

Like every morning in the SICU, Monday began with a chest X-ray to confirm that tubes were still properly placed and that there was no excess gas or symptoms of pneumonia in my lungs. All appeared to be normal with my heart too—a good start to my third full day in the SICU.

More good news followed. Both the Neo-Synephrine and the Dopamine were discontinued, and the IV in my right forearm was removed. Inside, I was jumping for joy. Each medication discontinued and IV removed were clear confirmations that I was healing. Sheri made certain that we gave out a hardy *woohoo* (albeit a feeble one from me) to celebrate each little victory. We were both astonished at how fast my body seemed to be healing given the devastation it had incurred. Even though I remained in a highly compromised state, every little bit of progress continued to fuel our hopes and our belief that a substantial recovery might be possible.

Around 10:00 a.m., Dr. Tominaga came in to see me during her rounds and was very encouraged by my improvements from the previous day. A dedicated doctor, she seemed to live in the SICU. Her presence always inspired confidence in me and my family. She made us feel as though I was receiving the best care on the planet.

Next, the speech pathologist dropped in to test me on more pureed food and thick liquids. I found swallowing had become more painful, but it was quickly fixed with a little morphine. She notified us that I would undergo something called the Modified Barium Swallow Exam (MBSE) later in the afternoon to see if they could upgrade my diet from puree and thick liquids. This was an exam I really wanted to pass. Any solid food, short of Spam, would mean more progress and would certainly taste better.

Around 11:30 a.m., Nurse Meg, my assigned case manager, paid us a visit for the first time. She let us know what we might expect over the next week or so. First, once I was stronger, I would be moved to a Patient Care Unit (PCU) bed and would share a room with one other patient. While the thought of losing what privacy I had was unsettling, I knew a transfer to the PCU meant I was getting better. Also, I would finally be able to sleep with fewer interruptions. Second, we should not be surprised if physical therapy and occupational therapy personnel became involved in my case in the near future. In addition, Nurse Meg said she would see me every day and stay on top of my case, which she did.

No sooner did she leave then Dr. Ammirati came by around noon for a follow-up visit during his rounds. He was pleased to see I was doing well and there were no complications from the embolization surgery. He tested my grip in both hands. My left was improving, but my right hand wasn't, and when I compared my left hand recovery to my right, I was concerned. My right side, from my shoulder down through my hand, seemed to have gotten the worst from the accident, second only to my spine. However, when I remembered the extreme burning sensation I had felt in my right hand at the accident scene, I was hardly surprised that it was lagging behind substantially.

Before he left, Dr. Ammirati assured us that the right vertebral artery would now present no risk during Dr. Leary's posterior cervical surgery on my C6 vertebra, scheduled for tomorrow. He gave us a reassuring smile and went off to visit his other patients.

Throughout the activity of the morning, Sheri and I had forgotten about the looming second spine surgery. Dr. Ammirati's visit, while pleasant and reassuring, was a reminder that more repair work needed to be done. Receiving mixed news such as this made for a bit of an emotional roller coaster.

At 1:30 p.m., I took the swallow test. I was given thick and thin liquids, mixed solids, and a cracker. The speech pathologist and attending physician observed how my body processed each, using a fluoroscope, which let them watch the food's path as I swallowed. While I was able to tolerate solids, I still aspirated thin liquids. It amounted to some progress and resulted in an order to continue the restricted diet, but with no liquids, including sauces, syrups, gravy, and soups. The standard American diet would have to wait.

JOHN MIKSA WITH SCOTT P. LEARY, M.D.

By 5:00 p.m., it was time for Dr. Leary to make his rounds. He checked for neurological improvement and found some in my lower extremities and my left hand. However, the weakness in my right hand persisted. Nevertheless, Dr. Leary was so pleased with my progress that he ordered physical therapy (PT) and occupational therapy (OT) to begin the next day, just as Nurse Meg had predicted.

Sheri and I didn't know exactly what PT and OT would look like, but orders to start it seemed like a real win to us. If that wasn't good enough news, he also informed us that he had decided to defer the surgery on my C6 vertebra until Wednesday. In fact, he now thought that he might not have to operate at all! This was super news and filled us both with a great deal of joy and hope. Sheri couldn't wait to tell Meg and Wes.

Later in the evening around 8:30 p.m., the nurse allowed Sheri to shampoo my hair. Mind you, it was with a specially designed, self-contained shower cap, which included the shampoo and moisture. There isn't much else you can do in the SICU with a neck brace and IVs. Still, it felt great and gave me back a sliver of dignity. After Sheri, Meg, and Wes had gone home, the nurse offered to give me a bath, which would have been terrific. By that time, though, the pain in my neck, right shoulder, and right hand had made moving too uncomfortable, so I opted out of the sponge bath.

Morphine quickly squelched whatever pain came along. As it began to provide relief, my mind could focus on other thoughts. On this night, I had a very motivating one in my head—I had turned a corner today. And tomorrow, I would continue on my road to recovery beginning with physical and occupational therapy.

AN EXHILARATING THIRTY SECONDS—TWICE

Just like clockwork, on Tuesday, my blood was drawn at 5:00 a.m. for routine laboratory tests, as it had been every day. My chest X-ray was completed around 6:00 a.m., and aside from a potassium deficiency, I passed both tests with flying colors.

Dr. Leary came by to see me around 9:00 a.m. during his usual morning rounds. After completing a brief neurological exam, he said I was doing "extremely well." I was feeling sensation in both my lower extremities, but my limited ability to move my legs and their lack of strength was of concern, as was my right lower arm, from my elbow through my hand. In fact, my right hand seemed to have a mind of its own, similar to that of Dr. Strangelove from the classic 1964 movie of the same name.

The nursing staff and Sheri all knew I was quite apprehensive about my upcoming physical and occupational therapy sessions. In my youth, I had been a multi-sport athlete, and I had continued to be physically active my whole life. The notion of training to get better had always set well with me, until now. I felt as weak as a newborn kitten and couldn't imagine what exercises they would pace me through that would be of any use. I managed to conjure up all sorts of negative fantasies, such as falling off the bed and re-breaking my neck.

At this point in my healing, my strength and coordination were diminished so much, I couldn't even feed myself. Although I felt sensation in many parts of my body, my motor skills and strength were all severely lacking. Further, I had no idea what these therapies meant relative to my condition. I wasn't about to jump out of bed, drop down, and give them twenty pushups (although I would have loved to, just to see their faces). I would just have to wait and see what the therapists had in store for me.

But before PT and OT, it was time for more speech and swallow testing. This time, we tried thick liquids, some puree, and a few varieties of soft, chopped solids. My throat pain had lessened, but the solids felt like they were stuck in my throat, so we ended the test. Another test was scheduled for five days hence, and I was to continue on my present (limited) diet—a disappointing result.

Dr. Tominaga, or Dr. T. as we came to call her, dropped in for a visit around 1:00 p.m. and told us she was a bit concerned with two things: my lack of sleep and my excessive use of morphine. Some of the motivation to transfer me to the Patient Care Unit was to address my sleep deprivation. Based on my present condition, however, Sheri was not at all keen to have me transferred anywhere just yet. That evening, she expressed her thoughts quite clearly to the night shift nurse, who passed Sheri's concern to the charge nurse. Sheri's advocacy was successful, and my transfer was postponed.

My morphine use was Dr. T's second concern. During my first full day in intensive care, Dr. T had coached me on the importance of getting rest and sleep to aid in my recovery. I had been trying to avoid narcotic painkillers for obvious reasons, but I needed the morphine on many occasions to relieve the breakthrough pain and help me rest. Although she wanted me to help manage my pain by accepting the morphine, Dr. T was beginning to think I was becoming too attached to it. As usual, she kept an eye on my daily consumption and switched me to Vicodin whenever appropriate. This switch seemed to help.

In preparation for my impending physical and occupational therapy, which would require as much mobility as I could muster, my drain from the spine surgery was removed. Frankly, I never noticed it. I can't say that about the ET and NG tubes. They were both extremely noticeable, in particular the ET tube. At least, it was gone—good riddance! The NG tube, however, was ever present and quite a nuisance. Every removal or discontinuation of a tube, IV, or medication represented a small victory, and yes, I was keeping score.

Finally, it was 2:00 p.m. and time to begin my first PT and OT sessions. My therapists were Lisa and Marissa, respectively, and when they approached my bedside, Lisa said, "John, what's your goal?"

My answer was as straightforward as her question. "I want to get better," I said.

At the time, I had no idea what "get better" really meant. How far would my body come back? Would I be able to walk on my own again? Would I regain use of my right arm and hand? Would my new internal hardware remain intact for a lifetime? In other words, how much of my pre-accident life could I achieve? I was very motivated to do whatever they asked, but I didn't know what my new reality could look like.

What a sight I must have been. I had virtually no strength, was sporting a hard Aspen neck brace, my NG tube dangled from my nose, I remained connected to multiple monitors, my catheter was still attached, and multiple IVs protruded from both arms and my chest. Compared to me, a marionette would have been more prepared for my first therapy sessions. At least, that's what I thought. My caregivers knew better.

We started with physical therapy. I had to sit before I stood, stand before I walked, and walk before I ran. My therapists began the process of testing my functional mobility for rolling, side lying-to-sit, sit-to-side lying, sit-to-stand, and stand-to-sit. After trying a few log rolls, I moved on to the side lying-to-sit exercise and back again. These very simple movements felt like I was trying to climb Mt. Everest. I fatigued quickly and, along with it, became discouraged. It took all of my self-motivation to keep a positive attitude.

With a few of those under my belt, I sat at the end of the bed. My job was to sit motionless by finding my midline, but while I thought I was staying upright, I kept falling to my left. I would have fallen completely over, if not for the therapists supporting my body. This seemingly insignificant task, to sit steadily at the end of my bed, and my performance or lack thereof, made it abundantly clear what might be in store for me with both physical and occupational therapy. I realized I had a very long way to go to return to normal.

Now, the big moment—the time had come for my first attempt to stand. With the help of two therapists and something called an Encore Machine, a hydraulic lift of sorts, I tried to go vertical. Only with the help of this machine and both therapists pulling up on my safety belt could I get to my feet. Once there, I felt weak, wobbly, unsure, quite anxious, and short of breath. In fact, I felt as if I had been hit by a car…

Nevertheless, with all their help, I stood for thirty seconds! After sitting back down on the bed and resting for a few minutes so my heart rate and blood pressure could recover, I got up again for another thirty seconds.

"Mark this day," I grinned at Sheri and Meg. "I stood again for the first time."

They were both beaming. "Way to go, Dad," Meg declared. Sheri looked at me and said emphatically, "Yes!"

In spite of this victory, the therapists' overall musculoskeletal evaluation confirmed that I had poor static sit balance, poor dynamic sit balance, and poor static stand balance. Humpty Dumpty was a star compared to me. However, the therapists were not disappointed. They had enough experience to know this was a good start, and they told us we should be encouraged. The therapy goal was clear—get me to the point where I could do all of the motions and tasks we had done today, every day, and by myself. I was tagged as being an excellent candidate for acute rehabilitation.

I wasn't sure how they arrived at that conclusion. I would have rated my performance as extremely poor. Without maximum assistance, I could not log-roll, sit up, stand up, or sit down. Then, again, I had only the "pre-accident John" to use as a baseline for comparison. On the other hand, my therapists were trained to see the possibilities. I decided to feed off their optimism.

Next up, we did my first OT evaluation, which included tests for occupational function, performance, and skills. The assessment results were predictable. I had a decreased ability to execute basic grooming/hygiene, dressing, bathing, toileting, showering, and self-feeding. Also, I was impaired in functional mobility, upper extremity function, energy conservation, activity tolerance, strength, and sensation. Other than that, I was good to go.

The treatment plan was for me to relearn and improve in all of these areas within an acute inpatient rehabilitation hospital. As I considered how long it would take to recover all of this lost strength, function, mobility, coordination, and skill, I started feeling overwhelmed. It was time to break this problem into smaller pieces. I knew I'd be most successful if I approached my road to recovery with a "one day at a time" attitude, mentally recording even the slightest progress. If nothing else, I now had very clear baselines from which to start.

What a journey this was going to be with a final destination unknown. But I was alive and my body was beginning to reconnect itself. I had the best partner possible in Sheri and support from family and friends. I had just stood for an exhilarating thirty seconds, twice, and I had not passed out. This was a milestone worth celebrating.

SORRY TO SEE YOU GO, BUT WE NEED THE ROOM

I knew I had physical and occupational therapy sessions planned for the morning on Wednesday, so I began to mentally prepare for them. At 11:30 a.m., my friendly therapists were back to see me, bringing along the Encore lift. I was determined to do better on my second day of therapy than I had on my first. When they asked me how I was doing, I said, "Great. Let's do this." At least, I knew what to expect this time.

Sure enough, my log rolling improved, and I could sit at the end of the bed while maintaining my midline for about five minutes, after which I got tired and began to wobble. Five minutes was five minutes, though, and worth celebrating!

Once the therapists moved the Encore into position and grabbed my safety belt, I managed to get off the bed and stood upright with maximum assistance on both sides. I completed two sets of this movement for about thirty seconds each, but hyper-extended my knees each time. When I tried to compensate for the bad technique, my legs buckled. With my expectations perhaps too high, I was disappointed. I supposed I was a bit too fired up and wanted to overachieve. I could see that progress would have to come in increments, not quantum leaps.

Switching to occupational therapy, we began to work on sit-to-stand exercises. After completing three sets at ten seconds each, we moved on to mobility work for my right upper arm and shoulder. The more I did with my right side, the more my nerves began to tingle and burn. Although uncomfortable, I was happy to feel my nerves beginning to re-engage. It reminded me of something my Marine Corps friends told me—pain is weakness leaving the body. The faster it left, the happier and stronger I would be.

Dr. T made her rounds around 1:00 p.m. and did her usual thorough exam. Again, she encouraged me to try the Vicodin in lieu of the morphine unless I was having unmanageable, breakthrough pain. Also, she informed us that I was being moved, probably late in the afternoon. I had graduated to a private room on the fourth floor!

"There," she said, "you will get much better rest."

I was all in favor of some decent shut-eye, and I was delighted to learn that I was considered well enough to be moved out of the SICU. It meant I must be getting better. This was yet another very welcome sign of progress.

Soon after Dr. T's visit, I had a brief visit from the speech therapist. Dry chunky food was still getting stuck in my throat, intensified by the presence of the NG tube, but Dr. T was unwilling to have the tube removed until she knew I could tolerate liquids. We would not know if I could do that until the completion of another swallow test, which wasn't scheduled until August 30. For now, the restricted diet would stay in place, and pureed food would have to do.

Dr. Leary came by around 3:00 p.m. and noted my increased posterior neck pain and the increased tingling and burning in my right hand. The neck pain concerned me the most, but neither Sheri nor I wanted another cervical spine surgery, much less one so close in time to the first. Even though it was Wednesday, the second spine surgery had not yet been scheduled. However, if it was needed, then so be it.

To influence his decision with regard to the second spine surgery, Dr. Leary wanted more data, so he ordered a four-position X-ray of my C5-C6 cervical spine area. After reviewing the results, he would make a final go-or-no-go decision, but so far, he thought the posterior surgery might not be needed and told us as much. Although it may have been premature, Sheri and I celebrated the good news.

The intensive care unit's rhythm had begun to pick-up around 5:00 p.m. I needed to be fed and prepped for my big move to my new digs on the fourth floor, so after saying good-bye to my fantastic nursing team in the SICU, I was rolled to the X-ray room for the C-spine series. Afterward, my family joined me as the orderly wheeled me on my gurney to my new home, Room 409.

Here, too, the nursing staff was friendly, professional, and attentive. They examined my IV and catheter and briefed me on the use of the call button and television.

I was then left to settle into my new, spacious, and very quiet room. I felt as if I'd just checked into the Presidential Suite at the Fairmont Hotel in San Francisco!

There was even a small sofa in the room near my bed. I'm not sure with whom Sheri pulled strings, but to my delight, she had arranged to stay the entire night, sleeping on the sofa. I awoke a couple of times during the night, expecting to be in the SICU, only to see her across my private room, sleeping peacefully. It was the best night's sleep I'd had since my arrival five days ago—what seemed like a lifetime.

THE SLIPPERY SLOPE OF MORPHINE ADDICTION

Awakening in a private room Thursday morning was an entirely different experience than doing so in the SICU. Although my body was only a few days into reconnecting its neurological pathways, and I had no more strength than a fragile hummingbird, for the first time since the accident, I felt out of danger. The transfer from the SICU to Room 409 had really boosted my morale, and I felt that my path to recovery, however long it might be, was much more achievable. Having breakfast (such as mine was) in the room with Sheri further enhanced my sense of normalcy, if you can ever achieve that feeling as a hospital patient.

Nevertheless, I still faced a huge uphill battle to maximize my recovery. One obstacle getting in my way was pain, both in my neck and especially in my right shoulder, arm, and hand. I would find out later what was causing the shoulder pain, but my right hand's tingling/burning sensation and weakness clearly was the result of nerve damage. Frankly, regaining the use of it was becoming as much a concern to me as the return of motor function to my legs.

Meanwhile, in the course of managing my pain to help me rest better, I had begun to slide down the very slippery morphine slope. I apparently was taking Dr. T's advice to control my pain a bit too far. More often than not, the pain was climbing up to the high end of the 0-10 scale. When asked, I would accept either 2.5 mg or 5.0 mg doses of morphine. And sure enough, the pain would disappear.

On her afternoon rounds, Dr. T addressed my use of morphine straightaway. "What's with the morphine, John? I thought you would use the Vicodin?"

"Well, the morphine seems to work really well, and you told me to get more rest by managing the pain."

After cautioning me on its narcotic powers, Dr. T instructed the nurses and me to stop using it except in extreme cases. She was not about to let me go any further down this dangerous slope. As of that afternoon, I was off the morphine for good.

Pain wasn't my only challenge. Sometimes, it took the form of managing simple bodily functions, such as urinating, which I was not yet able to manage on my own. So when my catheter decided to malfunction, it made quite a mess of me and my bed. This was the first time I began to consider what it might be like to be incontinent or impotent or both. Fortunately, a PT session was scheduled to start, which helped me refocus on something much more positive.

Right on time at 1:30 p.m., Jen and Ed, my two physical therapists for the day, arrived with a mission to amp up my PT. When they came into my room, I said to them, "What do I have to do today?" While they took my question as a complaint, it was anything but that. I was simply trying to understand what they expected from me. I still had very little strength and seemingly even less control of my body. If I was going to make up for the lack of physical strength with a positive mental attitude, I needed all the information I could get.

We started right in. After working my limbs and holding a sitting-up position, it was time to try standing. With the help of both Jen and Ed and the Encore machine, up I went. I managed to stay standing for two minutes before becoming fatigued. Unlike yesterday, I became lightheaded and broke into a sweat. It was not my best effort. They lay me down and checked my pulse and blood pressure. Both were fine, but they decided to call it a day.

I was really disappointed. I wanted so much to improve from the day before. I guess my brain was asking my body for more than it could handle. Nevertheless, Jen and Ed recognized that, over time, I could improve a great deal more, but only with the help of professional physical therapy. Consequently, they recommended me for acute rehabilitation. I had no idea what that meant, but if it would enable me to get better, then I was all for it.

When you have no experience being this injured and no experience witnessing someone else's recovery from a serious injury, you tend to fear going too far, too fast. While I desperately wanted to get better and was willing to do whatever therapy was required, I was convinced that I needed more time to gain strength before being transferred to acute rehab. After all, my idea of rehab included physical activity well beyond my current capabilities, and right now, I still needed someone's help just to sit up in bed and be fed. This hardly fit the description of someone ready for wind-sprints and grass drills.

I didn't understand that acute rehab for me would mean learning first how to sit up, lie down, and transfer from a bed to a wheelchair and back again. Becoming even partially ambulatory would be farther down the road.

To help mitigate my concerns about a transfer to acute rehab in what I thought was too early in my recovery, Rita, a representative from Scripps Memorial Hospital Encinitas Rehabilitation Center, paid Sheri and me a visit. She was quite pleasant and helped us to understand more fully what acute rehab would be like, specifically for me. After listening to Rita, Sheri had decided I should go to the Encinitas location for two reasons: continuity of care by staying in the Scripps system and its proximity to our home, which was only seven miles from the Rehabilitation Center.

Rita's visit helped relieve some of my anxiety about this next stage of my recovery, but I was still trying to negotiate with the SMH-LJ staff for more time to build up strength while staying in Room 409. Of course, the staff was having none of it and explained that the sooner I started acute rehab, the better off I would be. This was not their first rodeo. Clearly, they knew what medical treatment path would be best for me.

So, it was decided. Friday, August 28, was set for my transfer, just one week after my devastating accident.

The next day at noon, I would be taken by ambulance to Scripps Memorial Hospital Encinitas Rehabilitation Center to begin what was expected to be a very long stay, probably months.

That night, while Sheri helped me eat dinner, we talked about this next phase of my recovery. Neither of us had any idea of how much of my motor function would return. Would I be able to live independently? Walk again? Make love again? We decided that I would need to keep a positive mental attitude and try my best every day to improve. My new normal would be somewhere between quadriplegia and my pre-accident body. So much work lay ahead, but I knew what my goal would be. With so many prayers and so much support, how could I not achieve it?

Once dinner was finished, Sheri and I agreed that going home a bit earlier for her was a good thing. I assured her my left hand worked well enough to buzz the nurses if I needed their help, so she left to have a quiet dinner with Meg and Wes. Together, they contemplated the events of the last six days and gave thanks for the miracle they continued to witness.

Not long after Sheri left, Dr. Leary came by to see me at about 9:30 p.m. It took me a few moments to come out of a deep sleep I had fallen into before I recognized who was at my bedside. Once I did, it was like seeing a long-lost friend. I knew I would be under someone else's care at the rehab center starting tomorrow, so this would be his final visit with me on his rounds. He told me how well I was doing and that X-rays confirmed there was no need for a posterior cervical spine surgery, which sent my spirits soaring. After his brief visit, I recall him saying something cordial as he was walking out of the room. What I said in return was a raw emotional response and thank you for all he had done.

"Hey, Dr. Leary. Love you, man."

SEVEN DAYS TO THE MINUTE

My last morning at the hospital was very different from my first. Intubation was gone. I could speak. I could move my arms and legs. I had some degree of feeling all over my body. Only one IV remained. The leftover abject terror of the crash had abated. I was pathetically weak and could do very little for myself, but I knew I was getting stronger. I was filled with hope, determination, and anxiety about my future. I yearned to know how far and how fast I might recover. It was too early for anyone to know.

After all, in the span of just seven days, I had gone from total paralysis to emergency spine surgery and then vascular surgery, to looking forward to my daily sixty minutes of physical and occupational therapy. Maybe the occupational therapy was nothing more than trying to wipe my face with my left and right hands (the left was much more successful), bend my arms at the elbow, and move fingers as best as I could, but my body was trying to function. Even though I had experienced a great deal of nerve damage, muscle atrophy, and extreme loss of strength, compared to a week ago, I was in a far better place. My optimism soared. I was more than ready for the day's PT and OT.

Right on cue, my physical and occupational therapists arrived at my bedside around mid-morning. I knew it was vitally important to keep my progress moving forward, especially after yesterday's minor setback. So I welcomed Julie, Jen, and Ed with a robust "I'm going to do better today!"

After some mundane bed exercises, it was time to test my endurance for standing, first for two minutes and then for three. I couldn't wait. With maximum assistance from Jen and Ed as they gripped the safety belt around my waist, I positioned myself in front of the hydraulic lift. On the count of three, I stood for the first two-minute set. No problem. In fact, they had me shuffle my feet a few inches forward, then a few inches backward. It didn't qualify as walking, but it sure got my attention and gave me a rush of adrenaline.

I sat back down on the bed for a brief rest period before we launched into set number 2 with a three-minute goal. Ed called out the time milestones—one minute, one and a half minutes, two minutes. Once I passed the two-minute mark, I knew I had reached a new personal best and wanted to go the distance for three. To my delight, as well as Jen's and Ed's, I made it! I was thrilled. All I was doing was standing and doing an almost indiscernible shuffle, and with help from two therapists and hydraulics, but that didn't matter. My gosh—you would have thought I just won an Olympic gold medal for cycling time trials. There was only one glitch. Near the end of the three-minute set, I felt my left ankle pop and give way a bit. Although pain was absent, I knew something wasn't right, but I would have to wait a few days to find out just what it was. It didn't matter. I had just stood for a total of five minutes!

My elation soon gave way to being totally immersed in the hubbub of transfer preparation. The plan called for me to be discharged by noon and taken to the rehabilitation center by ambulance. By 11:30 a.m., Sheri and I both knew things were running a bit behind schedule. Nurse Meg tried to get me and my paperwork ready as soon as possible, but the ambulance EMTs, who had arrived already, would just have to cool their jets.

Dr. T wrote her final orders around noon, which included starting a new IV line in my left arm, removing the central line from my chest, and removing the stitches over my left eye. Sheri said she had totally forgotten about the gash over my eye and how dangerously close it had come to causing much more serious damage. I, too, had totally forgotten about it. We had much bigger fish to fry on our worry list.

Before being shipped out, Dr. T thought I should have a quick chat with a staff psychiatrist. At this point in my discharge process, tasks were being performed swiftly and efficiently with the objective of getting me on my way. Consequently, my psychiatric exam lasted only fifteen minutes.

I suppose a psychiatrist can glean something useful in a short period of time. However, given my highly compromised physical, emotional, and mental state, further enhanced by the heightened activity to get me on my way, I was not at all surprised when I became emotional while answering the doctor's questions. In hindsight, I probably should have politely refused the brief chat session. All of my thoughts and energy were being directed to what lay ahead for me at the rehabilitation center and beyond, which was still a big unknown. Getting in touch with my thoughts and feelings about what had happened to me and my outlook on the future, at that point in time, was not on my priority list. At least, he concluded, I wasn't crazy.

Finally, with my discharge papers in hand, the time had arrived. The boys from the ambulance company were called into Room 409 to facilitate my transfer to their gurney. With a "one, two, and shift," I was off on a new ride. Without further delay, we were headed down the hall and into the elevator. As an EMT pushed the main floor button and the doors closed, I held Sheri's hand with my left one. A strange sense of loss wafted over me. I was saying good-bye to countless professionals, some I had met and others I never saw, all of whom played some role in getting me this far. Yes, transferring was a huge milestone in my recovery, but I would miss those who had taken such good care of me for seven days.

When the elevator doors opened, we rolled straight to the exit door. Busting out into the afternoon's fresh, hot air and brilliant sunlight was a bit of a shock. In just one week, I had forgotten what it was like to be outside. An even bigger shock came when the EMTs opened up the back of the ambulance. It had been air-conditioned and ready to roll—over two hours ago.

Since then, it sat closed, locked, windows rolled up, and the engine turned off. Now, the temperature inside was about 120°F.

Fortunately, the rear double doors provided a quick escape for much of the heat. When the EMTs loaded me into the back, I was sporting an IV, nose tube, catheter, and neck brace. One EMT stayed in the back and sat to my left. Sheri climbed in and sat down to my right. As we pulled out of the parking lot, I asked her what time it was. She said, "It's 2:30 p.m."

The synchronicity of the moment struck us both simultaneously. Recalling what had happened exactly seven days prior, to the minute, we exchanged a deep, penetrating look. Neither of us said a word. What more could be said?

PART III

THE MIRACULOUS RECOVERY

GOAL #1: WALK AGAIN

SETTING THE BAR HIGH

Within the realm of neurological science, I had already made a stunning recovery. Some degree of feeling had been restored to most of my body. Motor function capability was beginning to return. What remained was a two-fold problem: I had virtually no strength, and my body needed to relearn every basic activity used in daily living. Having been quadriplegic just seven days prior from a complete spinal cord injury, my new rehab therapists knew they had their work cut out for them.

The question remained—how far would I comeback from this devastating injury? No one could and no one was willing to make a prediction. My caregivers' common goal would be to strengthen my body and to teach me how to complete basic "active daily living" tasks. I wasn't sure what I would be able to do again, but one thing was very clear in my mind. I wanted to walk again, unassisted. Everything else took a backseat to my #1 goal.

ARRIVAL AND CHECK-IN

We arrived at the admissions entrance to Scripps Memorial Hospital Encinitas Rehabilitation Center at about 3:00 p.m. on Friday, August 28. As I was removed from the back of the ambulance, the brilliant sunshine washing over my face, I squinted like a newborn. Once again, I was given a vivid reminder that I had been given a second chance at life.

Once inside the rehab center, the EMTs completed their paperwork and handed me off to an orderly and Lester, a certified nursing assistant (CNA), who was assigned to my team for the duration of my stay. Lester and I hit it off right away. He had spent six years in the navy as a corpsman and had dealt with many different patient cases. I would later discover that he had quite the droll sense of humor. The fact that his biceps were the size of my thighs was very helpful too. They would come in quite handy for the many boosts I would require, similar to those I had been given in the SICU, to get my head back to the top of the bed. A middle-aged man, Lester also had an abundance of interesting and useful life experiences, so nothing seemed to surprise him.

To supervise my arrival, Nurse Jackie quickly took charge. A diminutive woman with Hawaiian ancestry, her smile was broader than her height. The first thing she said to me was, "Welcome, John! Your bed is ready. You'll be in Room 160A." I honestly felt like I was checking into a five-diamond hotel. Nurse Jackie most definitely had the caring gene. Her energy level and constant smile seemed to melt away all of my anxieties about transferring to the rehab center.

Within thirty minutes, I was settled in with my NG tube, catheter, IV intact, and neck brace. During the next hour, Nurse Jackie briefed me and Sheri on all the rehab center's protocols, including use of the phone, use of the beeper to call the nurses' station, and the general workings of the place. One thing in particular I liked was my own whiteboard, strategically placed on the wall at the foot-end of my bed in full view. Written on it every day and at every shift would be the names of my nurse and CNA. It gave me comfort to know who they were, which allowed me to connect on a personal level. They became part of John's Team. In the days ahead, I would draw strength from their strength, hope from their hope, and optimism from their optimism.

SAY GOOD-BYE TO THE CATHETER

Around 5:00 p.m., I began to experience leaking from my catheter. It was distressing to be fifty-four years old and essentially wetting my bed. What really bothered me was the thought of being incontinent. The order was given to remove the catheter and monitor what happened next. To everyone's surprise and my extraordinary delight and relief, I remained continent. Although I hadn't yet felt much sensation in that region of my body, I was glad to be rid of another invasive tube. Just two more tubes to go and I would be free of them all.

With another milestone to celebrate, it was time for dinner. Normally, the staff encouraged patients to migrate to the dining room for breakfast, lunch, and dinner, but I was in no state to go anywhere that evening. I certainly couldn't walk, and my training for transfer to and use of a wheelchair wouldn't begin until the next day. Dinner in bed was my only choice.

Sheri, Meg, and Wes were still there and watched as I awkwardly tried eating with my left hand. The first spoonful of pureed something I tried to put into my mouth made a direct hit on my NG tube, hanging from my nose, and went flying. Apparently, I had grown so accustomed to the tube that I'd forgotten it was there. Sheri stepped in and held the tube out of my way. At least, my appetite was returning. Eating meant strength. Strength meant better physical therapy. Better physical therapy meant I would walk sooner. Perhaps it was way too simplistic a formula, but it helped me to remain focused on my #1 goal.

WHAT MIGHT HAVE BEEN

Shortly after finishing dinner, my roommate in bed 160B came back from the dining room and introduced himself. Jim was about my age and quadriplegic. There I was, face-to-face with a man in a wheelchair who represented what might have been my destiny, if not for a miracle. His large personality was only surpassed in size by his sense of humor. Jim had perfected the art of snappy chatter. From that moment to this day, whenever I have seen Jim or spoken to him on the phone, he has a permanent smile on his face and in his voice—this from a man who suffered a complete spinal cord injury from C2 to C7. Since his motocross accident in 2000, he has required 24/7 nursing care. After a setback with his pacemaker, Jim had come to the rehab center for a tune-up.

Jim gave me all the inspiration I could ever have wanted. Until research discovers a functional cure for transected and severely damaged spinal cords, Jim will remain quadriplegic. I had come so very close to a similar fate—now, another reminder of my second chance sat in his wheelchair, separated from me by only a thin curtain divider.

Not long after midnight, I got my second lesson on what it would have been like to be permanently quadriplegic. Jim required a great deal of attention to cope with the most basic needs, including biological functions that healthy people generally take for granted. As quiet as the nurses and CNAs tried to be when caring for Jim, I easily awakened from a very light sleep. I wasn't sure if I would be able to adapt to my new environment and get the rest I needed for recovery. However, it was hard to feel sorry for myself being witness to Jim's circumstance, needing 365×24×7 care and assistance. Just to start his morning took several hours of dedicated help.

Yet, there he was, jolly Jim with his big personality. I concluded that God sent him into my life to implant an indelible memory in me of just how close I was to this existence and how very blessed I was to be the recipient of such a profound miracle. I decided to give it more time before requesting a transfer.

ESTABLISHING A NEW BASELINE

The next morning, after another comical attempt at feeding myself breakfast, Sheri and I had the pleasure of meeting Dr. Lobatz, the director of the rehabilitation center. This refined looking, sixtyish neurologist radiated cheerfulness and optimism. Sheri and I exchanged a quick glance as if to say to one another, "He will do just fine, thank you."

On this first Saturday morning visit, he thoroughly examined me to establish a baseline of where I was in my recovery. He told us exactly what my rehabilitation therapy would involve. During every twenty-four-hour period, I would receive my medications (which now were down to eight from a peak of twenty-five). I would have physical and occupational therapy six days a week to help me relearn normal movement patterns and relearn how to complete regular daily living tasks so I could become independent and take care of myself. Physical and occupational therapists would work diligently to help me on a path to achieve the fullest recovery possible, although what that looked like, no one yet knew. Additionally, Dr. Lobatz said that I would learn how to negotiate architectural barriers, how to restore my balance so I could move safely in both open and confined spaces, and I would *learn how to walk again.*

I'd learn how to walk again? That was the first time Sheri and I heard anyone say those words. Although we both had thought them, neither of us had spoken them. Hearing those words spoken by Dr. Lobatz crystallized for us the most important reason why I was in rehabilitation—to walk again.

Finally, he also ordered speech therapy and a swallow evaluation to find out if I had any residual speech issues and if I could progress from eating pureed food and thick liquids to solid food and thin liquids. Ultimately, we all hoped I'd be able to eat normally—someday soon.

Eight days had passed since the accident, and I was becoming aware of other noncritical injuries my body had sustained. I still felt the most pain in my left ankle, right shoulder, and right hand. My back and neck pain, to my great surprise, was minimal. But then, the most painful areas made perfect sense since I'd been hit on my left side by the driver and landed hard on my right side and neck.

Along with being a great listener, Dr. Lobatz was a maestro at orchestrating the resources of the rehab center and the hospital. He also provided calm, clear-headed counsel and indicated to Sheri and me that I'd probably be staying with them for about two to three weeks. Finally, he suggested that we should begin to think about what changes we might need to make at home to accommodate my new condition. Until then, neither of us had given physical changes to our home any thought whatsoever. We were determined in our belief that my recovery would be complete, no matter how long it took to achieve it.

After he left, Sheri and I reviewed what Dr. Lobatz had said. What really caught our attention was when he said I would learn how to walk. Really? When? To what extent? He certainly wasn't expecting me to be in a wheelchair long-term, even though I still had not even learned how to transfer to one from my bed. We were also surprised by the doctor's estimated length of my stay. Given my present physical condition and how far I had to go simply to become wheelchair-capable, much less ambulatory, a few weeks seemed like very little time to accomplish it all.

However, because Dr. Lobatz said it with such confidence, Sheri and I took it as a very encouraging sign. Privately, we had assumed I'd be there for two to three *months*! I realized that I certainly had a lot of hard work ahead of me. No matter—our spirits were definitely uplifted. Was everyone here as positive as Dr. Lobatz, we wondered? We would soon find out they were, and then some.

INTRODUCTION TO INPATIENT THERAPY

After lunch, I was wheeled into an X-ray facility for what I hoped would be my last Modified Barium Swallow Examination. If results were positive, I could begin to eat more solid and regular food, consume real liquids, and, most of all, remove the NG tube. Unfortunately, my results were mixed, and for now, my diet would stay the same.

What followed was a urology consult. Luckily, since the removal of my catheter, I had remained continent, and they found no infections. This was a very good sign that my nervous system was slowly reconnecting. While I had a great deal of weird and continuous tingling throughout my body, this was more evidence of it awakening from the total paralysis. It felt similar to when your wake up and realize you had been lying on your arm and had cut off the blood flow. Once the flow returns, your arm begins to feel like pins and needles. My whole body felt that way. A week ago, I'd have traded the world to feel these unusual sensations, so I certainly wasn't going to complain now.

My first introduction to the occupational therapy team came around 3:00 p.m. Lisa, one of several therapists assigned to me, put me through her exam and found that all of my limbs worked to some degree, but I got tired quickly. With her help and Lester's, I sat up in bed and, with lots of assistance and a good deal of instruction and demonstration, I managed to transfer to my assigned wheelchair. However, I wasn't strong enough to release the brake on the right side, even with the help of my left arm. It didn't matter, because making it into the wheelchair felt like I had reached a whole new plateau of recovery. It was one more baby step to my ultimate goal—walking.

Also, Lisa introduced me to the golden rule for spinal cord injury patients: absolutely no bending, lifting, or twisting (BLT) under any circumstances! This was certainly an easy rule for me to adopt and easy to remember because of the hard plastic neck collar I wore continuously. And frankly, I was terrified of doing anything that might reinjure my neck. In fact, I was afraid of making any move that could cause a sudden recurrence of the paralysis. This fear would manifest itself in other ways in the days and weeks to come.

Now that I was safely in my new set of wheels, it was time for my first real shower since before the accident. I needed Lisa and Lester to help me transfer from my wheelchair to the shower chair, along with every bit of strength and effort I could muster—which wasn't much.

Next, off came my clothes. I'd long since put aside modesty in the hospital. With compassion and respect, Lisa gave me as much privacy as possible. After my neck collar was covered with plastic, she turned the water on and gave me the hand-held shower head. I took it with my left hand and held it so the water washed over my body, first on the front, then down my back. To my shock, I felt thousands of nerve endings being aroused. There was no pain. In fact, it was just the opposite. It felt as if I were being pelted by a million miniature marshmallows.

After lathering as best I could with the soap and wash cloth, I slowly directed the water over every part of me except my head and neck. It felt like a baptism and as if I were being reborn. Feeling every water droplet served as a profound reminder of the miracle God had granted me.

I watched as residual sweat and grime from my ride eight days ago swirled in soapy circles on the shower floor and went down the drain. I knew my body, mind, and spirit were getting better. This was the beginning of a process of washing away my fears of paralysis and loss of independence. I felt an overwhelming sense of hope, trust, and the belief that God had a bigger plan for my life. Not bad results from my first real shower since the accident!

The process of getting dried off, dressed, transferred in and out of my wheelchair and back into bed wiped me out. But after thirty minutes' rest, Jim, one of my physical therapists, arrived. It would be the first of many sessions together, and I was intrigued by his combination of seriousness and sense of humor. The first thing he reminded me of was the BLT golden rule, quickly pointing out that he wasn't referring to a sandwich. I knew we were going to get along just fine.

When it came to his work, Jim was all business. His first job was to teach me how to log roll to a sitting position and to transfer to my wheelchair and back to bed using proper technique. Primarily, his job was to help me improve my mobility, strength, function, and endurance. In fact, all of the physical and occupational therapists' missions were the same—get me functioning independently, as quickly as possible. This would require a heavy daily load of progressively difficult and challenging exercises for me. Now that I was fully immersed in this new environment, I found I was actually eager to get started.

My immediate task was to transfer to my wheelchair, navigate to the commode, and transfer to it. I needed maximum assistance from Jim and Lester for the transfer to get onto the throne. If that wasn't dramatic enough, I needed a third person, Nurse Charlotte, to assist me in emptying my bowels in the toilet by way of an enema. Nurse Charlotte had just introduced herself that morning as being one of several nurses assigned to me. Pleasant and professional, she performed the enema in such a matter-of-fact manner, it vanquished any chance for me to become embarrassed or discouraged. Completely exhausted, I needed all three to get me off the commode, into my wheelchair, and back into bed just in time for dinner.

Since I was beginning to swallow medications better, I asked Nurse Charlotte if the NG tube could be removed before dinner. She made a call to Dr. Lobatz, got the order, and said, "Let's take that thing out." She also said it might be a bit uncomfortable as she tugged on it. Then, with little fanfare, she grabbed the end of the tube dangling from my nose and proceeded to remove it.

Memories tend to get exaggerated sometimes, especially when trauma is involved. But I swear that Nurse Charlotte backed up across the entire length of the room (which, of course she didn't) before the tube was completely out of my body. What clung onto it would have provided ample fodder for twelve-year-old boys and their jokes. Suffice it to say, it did not look appealing.

She also managed to have the order written to remove the saline lock on my arm (the IV drip had already been discontinued), which had begun to really irritate me. So at about 5:30 p.m., eight days after the accident, I was indeed tubeless in Encinitas!

Dinner with Sheri, Meg, and Wes at my bedside never tasted so good, even though I barely stayed awake.

After taking the last bite, I said good night and was fast asleep before they left my room. I had been completely drained of energy from my first full day of therapy.

The next morning, things were pretty quiet. The hustle and bustle of patients and therapists engaging in PT and OT on Sundays was minimal and generally reserved for therapy that could not skip a day. I decided to use the tranquil time before breakfast to address an issue I could no longer avoid—another very restless night.

The caregiving that Jim, my roommate, required during the night and early morning hours became too disruptive for me to sleep through. I respectfully put in a request to be moved to another room, knowing full well there was a chance I might offend Jim, which I did not want to do. In two short days, I had grown very fond and respectful of him.

I made certain that his nurse allowed me to tell him the news. Before moving down the hall to my new room, 151A, I told Jim, "You're a great guy and I enjoy your company, but I've got to get some sleep. Your maintenance visits during the night and early morning just aren't working for me. Frankly, you should be allowed to have a private room. I mean no offense, but I've asked to be moved."

He smiled then laughed, said no offense was taken, and asked me, "Why did it take you two nights to figure it out?" A truly classy and unselfish response!

Sheri joined me for a bedside breakfast at about 7:00 a.m. I told her about my new short-term goal—to be able to transfer to and from my wheelchair without assistance so that I could go to the bathroom whenever I wanted.

"Why is that so important?" she asked.

"Because I want to be free of these plastic pee bottles!"

I knew I had a lot to learn and a lot of strength, balance, and coordination to recover before I would be able to jettison the portable urinals. Since I didn't have them at home and had no intention of needing them there, I wanted to be free of them in rehab. This led me to a bigger idea. If I didn't need something at home before the accident, then I was bound and determined to not need it once I was discharged from rehab. In my stage of recovery, to some, this would seem like a rather lofty goal. Sheri understood, though. She knew this simple concept would neatly define a successful rehabilitation.

Who better to tell us about my first two days of progress than Dr. Lobatz? He stopped by mid-morning to examine me. Afterward, he told us that the paralysis in my arms and legs was improving. I told him that my left ankle, right shoulder, and right wrist were causing a lot of pain. Compared to them, though, my neck felt good.

Dr. Lobatz was not surprised. He told us that my body was waking up and identifying other issues, but the fact that it was able to do so was a good thing. He ordered X-rays for all three areas of pain and promised he'd have them done later that day. On Monday, he would consult an orthopedist about the results. He wanted nothing to stand in my way to have the most effective PT and OT sessions possible.

Right after Dr. Lobatz's exam, my Sunday OT session began, lasting thirty minutes. I received help and instruction on dressing myself, coping with my current condition, and setting expectations for my occupational therapy rehab. With the time remaining, we worked on some hand stretches, strengthening, and coordination. Clearly, my right hand was my biggest concern. At the time, I owned a very small cell phone, the feature-phone variety, which fit in the palm of my hand. To give you a sense of my right hand and arm baseline strength, I could barely hold the phone in my hand, much less perform a curl using my bicep—the phone weighed just 3.4 ounces. The last eight days had truly taken their toll.

Physical therapy began that afternoon at 2:00 p.m. and lasted thirty minutes. Jim had me work on bed mobility, log rolling to get to a sitting position, transferring to my wheelchair and back to the bed, and finally, moving about in the wheelchair. I had asked Jim to remove the footrests at the base of it. This allowed me to use my legs to propel myself forward by putting my heels on the floor and pulling them toward me. I wanted to get my cycling legs back and was willing to use anything to my advantage to accelerate the process. That day, I managed to move 150 feet in the chair with moderate assistance—a good start.

While the physical exertion during my PT was minimal, it completely wore me out. I was bereft of stamina. By dinnertime, I hardly had the energy to chew and swallow. This was becoming a pattern. Sheri, Meg, and Wes would come to my room to spend a little time with me at the end of the day, but it was all I could do just to stay awake. Because of my full PT and OT schedule, it only made sense for them to visit me at breakfast and dinner time. Even so, someone was always there to cheer me up and provide words of encouragement. What a joy and uplifting feeling it was to have my family by my side during those special visits.

Once they left for the evening, sleep came easily. It was a good thing, too, because the next day would be my first full schedule of therapy—five hours of intense, back-to-back sessions. Was I ready for this?

ASSESSING COLLATERAL DAMAGE

Monday morning, August 31, I had breakfast in bed again. I began feeling disappointed that I wasn't able to wheel myself to the dining room. It seemed as if everywhere I looked, I had more goals.

Dr. Lobatz made his rounds at about 7:30 a.m. with the results of my X-rays. Apparently, I had a slight fracture along the outside of my left ankle. The pop I had felt when standing with the Encore hydraulic machine three days ago in the SICU was an indication of collateral damage from the accident. Frankly, I wasn't surprised that something else was broken. I was surprised my ankle was the only other thing, given how hard I had been impacted by the car, bounced off it, tossed into the air, and slammed onto the road. I had no time to dwell on it, though, because PT was about to begin in earnest.

My sessions began on the hour and would last forty-five minutes. After a fifteen-minute break, they would start up again. Jim, Maria, and Dani formed the core of my PT team. Sessions began simply enough—lying on a large mat while my legs were manipulated and stretched in various ways. This required me to be in the gym with a dozen other people with a wide array of afflictions and injuries. Before seeing those other patients, I thought mine was the most serious rehab case in the center. Then I looked around. A number of other people in the gym actually seemed to be much worse off than me. It was a humbling experience.

Some of my first PT sessions did not happen in the gym. Back in my room, Jim proceeded to put me through a variety of bed drills and transfer techniques to and from my wheelchair. He explained that I would have to learn the physics that applied when I was rolling, standing, sitting, and transferring. Without a fundamental understanding of the proper techniques to complete these maneuvers, once instinctively known by my mind and body, I would limit my ability to make them what they were before my accident—second nature. Jim and all the rest of my therapists would cut no corners.

GIVE HIM THE BOOT

Finished with morning PT, Dr. Nichols, an orthopedic surgeon, was at my bedside. The battery of X-rays Dr. Lobatz had ordered revealed not only the slight fracture of my left ankle, but also a traumatically induced impingement syndrome of my right shoulder (medical speak for restricted movement usually accompanied by pain and discomfort) and arthritis in my right thumb aggravated by the crash impact.

Dr. Nichols suggested I begin to wear a Cam boot that would reach up and over my left calf. This would support my ankle and allow me to do weight-bearing activities for physical and occupational therapy. I wanted nothing to impede my ability to maximize my PT and OT sessions, so on went the boot.

As to my shoulder injury, he suspected rotator cuff damage, but said an MRI would be necessary to diagnose it. Since other issues had higher priority while in the rehab center, we both agreed that an MRI would wait until I was discharged. Having this hanging over my head was unpleasant, but I had bigger fish to fry, like trying to walk again. I did receive a shot of corticosteroid for my shoulder pain, which provided some welcome relief.

OCCUPATIONAL THERAPY RAMPS UP

For the next forty-five minutes, I worked on trying to regain feel and function in my right hand. I was very concerned about whether or not it would ever be usable again. Several occupational therapists would be putting me through stretching exercises and various activities using clothespins, pegboards, therabands, theraputty, digiflex, pullies, buddy bands, a thumb splint, adaptive equipment, and my favorite, the clam digger.

The clam digger was a simple yet clever device to help wake up the countless nerve endings in my hands. It was a box filled with dried beans, and mixed in with them were various items like bolts, coins, jacks, small rubber balls, marbles, and rings. Sitting and eventually standing in front of the box, I had to stick my hand into the beans and then locate and identify an item while keeping my eyes closed.

I easily completed the task with my left hand, but I found that using my right hand produced shocking results: my hand, surrounded by the beans, felt as if it was being stuck with a million pins and needles. Equally upsetting was the fact that I could not distinguish a bean from anything else. I wondered if I would have to become left-handed.

Avi, one of my occupational therapists, coached me during clam digger exercises and never let me get discouraged. He reminded me repeatedly that it would take time for my body to reconnect itself. Like other members of my therapist team, Avi was a constant source of encouragement. They expected me to excel at all of my tasks and told me as such.

Other occupational therapy activities I needed to relearn included dressing, tying shoes, writing, bathing, toileting, energy management, and coordination. The focus for physical therapy would be log rolling, transfers, leg and hip exercises, squats, bed mobility, sitting to standing, standing to sitting, sitting balance, and standing balance. All of these activities were precursors to more advanced exercises, leading to the ultimate goal—walking!

STANDING WITHOUT HYDRAULIC ASSISTANCE

Soon after lunch, Jim had me back in the gym for more physical therapy. Using the large mat, he began to instruct me on how to stand and how to sit back down. It seemed like light-years from my first attempt to stand in the SICU. Today, I only had help from Jim as he used the gait belt around my waist to assist me—no Encore machine and no second therapist. Amazingly, I stood up from a sitting position a dozen times. This seemed like a huge leap in progress, which I wasn't expecting so soon. The one thing holding me back was the constant fear of losing my balance during one of the sitting or standing maneuvers. What if I fell and broke my neck? The fear of being totally paralyzed again still haunted me, and I constantly tried pushing it out of my mind.

Fortunately, I was never in danger. All of the staff had my safety in mind, first and foremost. My gait belt was on at all times and either in their grasp or just a hair's breadth away. Nevertheless, my fear would begin to subside only when I felt more capable and confident in myself.

That afternoon, my family and I were given counseling on what to expect with my recovery and what I'd need so I could function at home. Since our initial discussion with Dr. Lobatz, we hadn't given the subject much thought. Clearly, the more physical capabilities I could recover, the less daunting the transition would be. Not surprisingly, it was after this counseling session when my obsession with walking multiplied a thousand fold. I could feel my legs getting stronger, and I was standing for longer periods of time. I was now using my heels and legs to propel me forward in my wheelchair. Throughout dinner with my family and afterward, as they wheeled me through the courtyard garden, I spoke of walking and nothing else.

My spirits were high as I got back in my bed for the rest of the evening. I told everyone who came by that I was going to try to walk tomorrow, and they all encouraged me. They also tried to keep my expectations realistic. With the side-rails on my bed raised up and my call button and urinal at my side, my family headed home, leaving me to my thoughts of what I wanted to accomplish tomorrow.

But those side rails, while up for my safety, made me feel trapped. They needed to come down. Another goal was in my sights—and I intended to achieve it.

MARIA, I WANT TO WALK TODAY!

Before going to sleep, I had multiple conversations with the evening staff about reaching my goal of trying to walk the next day. When I awoke at 3:30 a.m. after five hours of sleep, I picked up right where I had left off. Nurse Linda was the lucky recipient this time as she listened to my incessant declarations about me walking. She responded with encouragement and an appropriate amount of expectation management. After all, just eleven days prior, I'd been paralyzed from the neck down with a complete spinal cord injury.

My day was finally beginning. Right on time at 6:00 a.m., the lab technician arrived to take my blood sample. Normally, her early morning mission bothered me, but this morning I was too focused on and too motivated by my goal of walking to care. Even if it was just down and back between the parallel bars one time, I knew I would feel like I'd just climbed Mt. Everest.

Transfers to my wheelchair were getting easier as my strength increased. By now, I only required minimum assistance for transfers. Once in my chair, I would drag myself into the bathroom to try brushing my teeth with my electric toothbrush (which helped greatly) and washing my face, which was another story. Because feeling, strength, and coordination were still lacking in my right hand, trying to lather a washcloth with soap and water was at once frustrating and comical.

This and other experiences I had during my first week in the rehab center opened my eyes and heart to the plight of paraplegics and quadriplegics. My brief time of living life within the confines of a wheelchair with severely compromised strength, mobility, and endurance made me all the more empathetic. I could only imagine what these folks must endure on a daily basis and how very lucky, very blessed I was.

After finishing with my morning hygiene as best I could, I wheeled myself out to the courtyard garden. This became a morning ritual for me. Because of the early morning hour, I always had the courtyard to myself, which allowed me to reflect on my circumstance and to pray for the strength to fully recover. I marveled at how close I had come to transecting my spinal cord. Even so, my complete spinal cord injury should have rendered me quadriplegic—yet there I was, striving to walk again that day.

From the courtyard, I headed down to the dining room to join Jim and other rehab patients for breakfast. Sheri joined us and contributed some fresh brewed Seattle's Best Coffee from home. Thankfully, my diet had been upgraded to thin liquids, which meant coffee was now fair game. That was my first cup-a-Joe from home, and boy, did it taste great. For many reasons, it would be the best I ever had. The entire breakfast was the best I'd eaten in eleven days, and throughout it, I bent Sheri's ear about wanting to walk. She, too, tried to manage my expectations. She was concerned that because I was so hyped up to get this done, I might be terribly disappointed if I didn't succeed. She had become ultra-protective of me.

Once breakfast was over, Sheri escorted me back to 151A. Because of my maniacal focus on my recovery, after breakfast each morning, Sheri would "kick herself out" for the day. Once she left this morning, I had about thirty minutes in my room alone before the start of my first physical therapy session. I used the time to think about what I had hoped to accomplish, and walking was number 1 on my list. When Maria came to get me at 9:00 a.m. to take me to the gym, I was ready to go.

On the way down the hall, we engaged in the usual small talk as she checked in with me to gauge my physical strength and emotional state. Once in the gym, I was surprised by what she said.

"John, what do you want to do today?"

Turning to the parallel bars and pointing in their direction, I answered, "Maria, I want to walk today!"

"Are you certain?"

"Yes, I am. I want to walk. I need to give it a try. I think my legs are strong enough."

With her encouragement, I positioned my wheelchair at one end of the parallel bars and prepared to stand up, but in my haste, I had forgotten the proper technique to get to a standing position. Because my chest was not far enough over my knees, I only managed to get about halfway up before dropping back down, unceremoniously, into my wheelchair.

We both knew why I didn't make it upright. Before Maria could tell me to try again, I was already on my way up. This time, I made it. While favoring my left side with the boot, I steadied myself between the parallel bars with my arms and hands. I stood at the end for a minute or two, letting my body find its balance and my blood pressure stabilize. Maria assumed her stand-by assist position with her hand near my gait belt. Then, I took my first step.

I will remember those first steps using the parallel bars for the rest of my life. The more steps I took, the more I wanted to keep going. Observing my endurance closely, Maria let me go down and back inside the parallel bars multiple times for a total of 200 feet! The adrenaline was coursing through me. After about twenty minutes of walking, exhilaration and exhaustion took hold of me. I saddled up in my wheelchair, and we headed back to Room 151A.

I had about fifteen minutes before my occupational therapy session started, which gave me time to try and understand the significance of what I had just accomplished. Why was God giving me this second chance that many others would not enjoy? Could it really be only eleven days since my accident? Would I recover completely, or would my "new normal" look more like today? Was Dr. Pettit right—would I recover 100 percent? Is this truly a miracle?

I knew I needed more time to fully understand this gift from God, and I was humbled and amazed by what had happened in the gym that morning. If I could walk again, even if it meant with impairment, the future of my life, as well as Sheri's, would brighten immensely. Maybe some sense of normalcy would be achievable. I wanted desperately to get my life back, and on that September 1 morning, I had walked 200 feet closer to it.

My time of reflection ended abruptly with the start of thirty minutes of occupational therapy, followed immediately by a PT session with therapist Jim. We headed out of my room and down the hall toward the gym. As I heel-dragged myself in my wheelchair with Jim walking beside me, he told me he'd heard about my little walk earlier in the morning. I told him how pumped up I was and looked forward to working with him on more sit-to-stand, stand-to-sit, and balance exercises.

To my surprise, Jim asked me if I thought I was strong enough to walk some more. I jumped at the chance and said, "Absolutely!"

As I turned my wheelchair toward the parallel bars and began to move toward them, Jim said, "Where are you going?"

"Well, I thought you wanted me positioned at the end of the bars so that I could stand up and then walk."

"You're going to walk, but not using those."

As he pointed to the hallway, he said, "You're going to walk out there, in the hall. And because I think you can do it, you're not going to use a walker. I'll be there to give you all the stand-by and contact assistance (his hand actually touching my gait belt) you'll need."

I'm all for stretch goals and miracles, but this seemed way out of reach. But if Jim thought I could do it, then by God, so did I! This time, I stood up from the wheelchair in one motion on the first try. After steadying myself, Jim and I set out toward the rehab center main hallway and passed the nurses' station. If you can imagine Frankenstein trying to walk after downing one too many beers, I am certain that is what I looked like.

I blurted out to Jim, "Am I doing okay?"

"You're doing fine, just keep a nice, slow, even pace," he said confidently, always with his arm and hand close by my gait-belt, ready to provide any assistance, if needed.

We made our way up and down the hallway and finally back to my wheelchair in the gym, by which point I'd logged another 250 feet. We even fit in a few minutes of practice for proper sitting and standing before heading back to Room 151A. Once there, I transferred into bed, totally exhausted, but high as a kite.

After a quick thirty-minute rest, I went down the hall in my wheelchair to the dining room to join my lunchmates. Word had already spread about my first successful attempt at walking. The biggest pat on the back came from Jim, my quadriplegic ex-roommate. Although exuberant, a part of me felt guilty because Jim may never experience what I had just experienced, yet he was as thrilled for me as I was for myself. For the rest of my rehab stay, Jim continued to be one of my biggest cheerleaders.

Exhilarated but exhausted, I decided to take a nap before dinner. Before going to sleep, I telephoned Sheri to let her know I had walked 450 feet. I thought she was going to jump through the phone as she shouted out a very loud *woohoo!* She was thrilled beyond belief. We both were, and without saying it, we knew the implication—a normal life might, in fact, be possible.

That evening, Sheri, Meg, and Wes came to visit at dinner time. Rather than use the dining area, we chose a small library room just off the main hallway. It provided a quiet and intimate setting for me to describe what had transpired in my physical therapy sessions. As I spoke of my walking adventure, their faces lit up with joy. No one could hold back the tears. Every prayer they had said for me had been answered. Their initial meeting with Dr. Tominaga the afternoon of August 21, when they received the shocking news of my spinal cord injury and total paralysis, was still a very fresh and vivid memory. Compared to that conversation, what they heard from me in the library seemed truly miraculous.

After I finished telling my story, Meg handed me a card. I opened it and began to read the note inside congratulating me on walking again, curiously

JOHN MIKSA WITH SCOTT P. LEARY, M.D.

handwritten in crayon. I savored every word, but was confused by the signature. It read, "Love, Meg, Wes, and Baby Wright."

Suddenly, I understood its meaning—Meg and Wes Wright were telling me that she was pregnant with our first grandchild! To be given such wonderful news on the same day I walked again for the first time was beyond remarkable. A shower of positive emotions drenched us. We formed a group hug and, through our tears of joy, gave thanks for our many blessings.

REGAINING WHAT WAS LOST

I had no time to rest on my laurels. My first day of walking was fantastic, but I was still confined to my wheelchair whenever I wanted to go from point A to point B on my own. Fortunately, by the time I was nearing the end of my first week of inpatient rehab, I had gained enough strength and mobility that I could transfer from my bed to my ride without any assistance. Down came the side bars on my bed—victory!

The first day I was granted this freedom, I felt like an escapee. No longer would I just lay in my bed waiting for the next PT or OT session to begin. I would get out of bed, into my wheelchair, and was on the move, wandering all about the rehab unit. Using the heels of the Cam boot on my left foot and the running shoe on my right to propel me forward, *my clop-clop-clop* approaching sound became all too familiar to the staff. Best of all, moving like this made my legs, arms, and core stronger and readied me for the more challenging therapy work that was about to begin.

WEEK 1 OF INPATIENT REHAB ENDS

On Friday, September 4, my PT and OT sessions were deferred to the afternoon. That morning, the main event was what Dr. Lobatz called the family meeting. At about 10:30 a.m., Sheri, Meg, Wes, and I assembled into the rehab conference room. Chairing the meeting was Dr. Lobatz. Filling out the room were representatives from nursing, social work, the lab, PT, OT, radiology, speech therapy, the pharmacy, and even the cafeteria. Dr. Lobatz went around the room to get a briefing on my progress in each of the areas. He also wanted to understand what the plan was for the coming week and what the benchmarks for success would be. After asking me what I thought about my experience and progress to date, the meeting turned to the goal of my discharge.

In a perfect world, I might have stayed for another two to four weeks. This would have given me daily and hourly exposure to increasingly intricate and difficult PT and OT challenges. The goal was to get me well enough to reenter my own home environment. However, I needed to make the transition safely and successfully. While my progress had been rapid, I still had mountains to climb and valleys to cross to be ready for discharge. Regardless of these challenges, Tuesday, September 15, became my target for release from the rehab center—just eleven days away. That date seemed only a very short time away to me. But if that was the date, then I wanted to beat it. My birthday was September 14. I wanted to be home by then.

When I first arrived at the rehab center, Sheri and I were thinking my stay would be two or three months. Now, we had our sights clearly set on getting me home after just two weeks. Another lofty goal had been set.

PHYSICAL THERAPY GETS MUCH TOUGHER

Walking like I had consumed one too many adult beverages, fitted with a gait belt and therapist by my side to catch me, was not going to cut it in the real world. I had a long ways to go before achieving walking independence. To get there, my PT sessions had to become more varied and more intense.

Consequently, my PT team of Jim, Maria, and Dani began to expose me to a whole new range of exercises. Jim introduced two new things—sidestepping and changing direction. These drills got my attention. Walking in a straight line with my Cam boot was one thing. Now I was doing something requiring more agility and balance. I had to keep pushing the fear of falling and reinjuring my neck out of my head. With Jim's expert assistance, though, thoughts like these quickly evaporated from my mind.

The distances I walked began to get longer. First 500 feet, then 750, and soon I was surpassing 1,000 feet a day. No longer was I walking just the flat hallway of the rehab unit. My strolls were taking me all around the inside of the hospital, out to the uneven courtyards, and onto the gently sloping front lawn.

Dynamic balance drills became a part of daily life, too. Maria introduced me to the balance board, a piece of wood with a one-foot diameter cylinder attached to the underside of the board at its middle. When the cylinder was placed on the floor, my job was to step onto the wood and stay balanced by keeping the board parallel to the ground. Each day, as my equilibrium and balance improved, I was able to stay on the board longer without grabbing the parallel bars.

Even more exciting were the forward and backward practice falls Jim had me do. After leaning in either direction with my feet together, my job was to break my fall by stepping forward or backward. I was never in any danger since Jim and an assistant were placed on either side of me. Nevertheless, perhaps more than any other rehab exercise, this one grabbed my attention the most. It took a great deal of mental willpower to push the thought of breaking my neck out of my thoughts while doing this exercise. But as my confidence in my ability increased, those thoughts became less of an issue. It and all of the rest of the rigorous PT was preparing for reimmersion into the world I once knew. But I was nowhere near ready yet. Among other things, I needed to relearn how to navigate stairs.

That assignment went to Jim. He seemed quite motivated that afternoon, knowing this would be a big hurdle for me. Sheri happened to be in the rehab center, too, so Jim asked her to come along to watch my session. Neither of us knew what Jim had in mind until we walked to the end of the hall and entered a stairwell.

Pointing to the stairs, Jim said with a mischievous grin, "It's time to relearn how to use these."

"Are you sure I'm ready for this? After all, I'm still hobbling around in this cumbersome boot."

"You're absolutely ready. Let me show you how it's done."

Instructing me to keep a hand on the rail (which made me recall Avi's advice to always "keep a hand on the boat") and put my chest out over my feet, with Jim at my side, I was to ascend a full flight of stairs step by step. That is to say, I took a step up with one foot and landed the other foot on the same step. Once at the top of the stairs, I repeated the process on the descent.

Next, we went up the stairs step over step. This is the normal way you would think of someone going up a flight of stairs. Coming down step over step was the hardest of the four sets. The height differential caused by the Cam boot required me to be absolutely focused on my balance and the proper technique Jim had just taught me. To my heavenly delight, the stair drill was much easier than it looked. Knowing we had stairs at home, I now was confident I could manage them and would be able to sleep in our bedroom on the second floor. There would be no need for a temporary bed downstairs, thank you very much.

Later that afternoon, Sheri told me her heart stopped a few times while watching me go up and down the stairwell. The "going vertical" experience was a bit thrilling for me too. Jim, however, was a tower of confidence. I likened it to a trapeze artist working with a net. Not once did I feel I was in danger.

FREE TO WALK ANYTIME, ANYWHERE

By now, my occupational therapist team of Lisa, Avi, and Audrey had me dressing, showering, shaving, and even tying my shoe. Thanks to constant stretching and strengthening exercises, my right hand began to blossom. I could print somewhat legibly and use it to feed myself. Even the clam digger no longer defeated me. Active daily living tasks were becoming second nature.

Physical therapists Jim, Maria, and Dani amped up the difficulty and duration of my sessions. Walks became much longer as we made our way throughout the hospital and rehab center. Since the outside was no longer off limits, I walked on a wide variety of grassy knolls and undulating sidewalks. It seemed as though every step lit up my senses. I had never felt more alive. Once my ankle healed enough to jettison the Cam boot, I walked faster and faster. I never wanted these PT sessions to end. Walking meant progress. Walking meant healing. Walking meant freedom. Walking meant living a normal life again.

The day finally came when a very special medical order was written. On September 7, after completing morning PT and OT sessions, therapist Jim came to my room with an official-looking document. He handed it to me and suggested that I read it out loud. As the words rolled off my tongue, my ears were in disbelief—I had been given permission to walk anywhere in the rehab center anytime I wanted, without an escort. I simply had to observe patient privacy rules.

After Jim left my room, I held the medical order in front of me and just stared at it. To be allowed, and more importantly, to be able to walk freely anywhere I wanted was an amazing milestone. I had begun this unplanned journey as a quadriplegic at the accident scene. Now, I stood in Room 151A staring at a medical order tantamount to a graduation diploma, only this one represented much higher stakes. Memories of the last seventeen days filled my thoughts. I was on cloud nine.

OVERCOMING SETBACKS

Few things in life go exactly according to plan and seldom progress in a straight line. So, too, was the case of my recovery and inpatient rehabilitation. My first encounter with a setback in rehab occurred a few nights after my arrival. It was about 11:00 p.m., and I should have been asleep, but something was troubling me deeply. I asked Nurse Aida if she could stay for a while so I could share what was on my mind. She agreed, and I began to tell her my concerns.

I noticed that it was becoming harder and harder to fall asleep. I had developed a fear of awakening the next morning completely paralyzed, having twisted my neck during the night. Even though I wore the sturdy Aspen collar while I slept, which did a perfectly good job of immobilizing my neck, my fear persisted.

Nurse Aida listened to me compassionately. Then, she shared with me a recent dream she had had about dying and how she had asked God to help her stay alive so she could continue her work as a nurse. When she awoke, the dream had seemed utterly real to her. She believed the message being delivered to her in her dream was to trust God and believe in his kindness and mercy. She suggested that it was time for me to strengthen my faith and trust God even more.

After Nurse Aida left my room, I thought about what she had told me. It was nursing at its best as she displayed extraordinary empathy. I slept great that evening, absent any fear. She had helped me achieve peace of mind about my condition—a peace which remains with me to this day. I have never again had a single thought of my paralysis returning.

A few nights removed from that mental and emotional setback, I ran headlong into a physical one. At one o'clock in the morning, unable to sleep, I transferred into my wheelchair and headed down the hall to visit the nurses at their station. Before long, I was joining them while they were having their "night shift" lunch. I ate a cup of pudding from the nurses' secret stash and rinsed it down with some iced tea.

While hanging out in my wheelchair, my shoulder pain had flared up. To provide relief, I was given a dose of Tylenol and Tramadol, the latter being an opioid pain killer and muscle relaxant. When I took the Tramadol, I could hear Dr. Tominaga in my head, saying, "John, be careful with the narcotic painkillers." Finally, just before 2:00 a.m., the pain subsided. I had become quite tired by then, so I headed back to Room 151A and went to sleep.

Soon afterward, a combination of the pudding, water, iced tea, and Tramadol overwhelmed my bladder. At about 2:30 a.m., I awoke with a start, realizing I had just wet the bed. I was utterly shocked and completely embarrassed by what had just happened. While in the hospital, I had observed the complexities faced by patients living with incontinence. I was extremely grateful that I was continent, despite my terrible spinal cord injury. Suddenly, my condition had changed.

I reached for the call button and Nurse Thor answered. I told him what had just happened, and quickly, Nurse Dee and Salicia, my CNA on duty, were at my bedside. Needless to say, I was very upset. My initial reaction was to view this incident as a major setback. As both of them began the process of changing the bed and helping me into a gown, they explained why the incontinence happened. It was reasonable to assume that the overhydration, especially with the iced tea, combined with the Tramadol, a muscle relaxant, was too much for my bladder to handle. They both felt that the incident would be an isolated one, and with some simple hydration management, it would not happen again.

After being helped into the shower, I sat on the shower chair, leaned back against the wall, directed the warm water over my body, and emotionally lost it. It wasn't because of this isolated incident, but rather because it was a vivid reminder of the accident, the surgeries, SICU, rehab, the effects on my family, and the lasting impact the whole experience would have on us all. It was one huge emotional pig pile. Before I finished rinsing off the soap, I promised myself I would make lemonade from this bucket of lemons, although I wasn't sure at that moment how exactly I would do it.

MORE RECOVERY MILESTONES

NO LONGER NEEDED

The morning after receiving clearance to walk at will, I awoke to see my wheelchair stationed at the end of my bed against the wall. It brought a large smile to my face and a deep sense of tranquility and thankfulness, knowing I would not be spending the rest of my life in one. The time had come to say good-bye to this old friend. My ride had served me well, but I no longer needed it. I called the nurses' station to let them know I was awake and dressed and that I had something for them to take away.

When Jennifer, the CNA on duty, arrived in my room, I pointed to the wheelchair and said, "I won't be using this anymore."

She smiled, unlocked the brake, and took the wheelchair away. What stayed behind were my recent memories of its use and my abundant appreciation for my life and regained mobility. My quad friend, Jim, came to mind, as well. So, too, did the time at the accident scene when I felt myself becoming paralyzed and was so unsure of my future. But there I was, a little over two weeks since being injured, having relearned how to walk and no longer needing a wheelchair. I was just beginning to fully appreciate the magnitude of this miracle God had bestowed upon me.

A REVISIT FROM AN ANGEL

By the middle of my second week of inpatient rehabilitation, my physical therapists had me walking sideways, backwards, braiding, slaloming, and overlapping. I couldn't get enough. My energy had returned so much, that between PT and OT sessions, I'd leave my room and just walk, which is exactly what I was about do the morning of September 8. Just as I walked out the door, headed to the cafeteria, Sheri appeared out of nowhere right in front of me. Before I could even say hello, she said, "John, look who is here to see you!"

Her comment was puzzling to me. I had no idea who she was talking about. I wasn't expecting her, much less any other visitors that morning. She took my arm and led me out into the rehab hallway.

"My God, it's Brooke!" I shouted.

Instantly and instinctively, we closed the few paces of distance between us and embraced. Tears of joy and elation filled our eyes. The last time I had seen Brooke was eighteen days ago while she held my head as I lay on the street paralyzed and terrified. Now, here I was, standing and walking on my own, and fully able to give and receive the best of hugs.

I had about twenty minutes before the start of my next OT session, so the three of us went down to the dining room to continue our reunion. Brooke, who is a musician, asked if Sheri and I would mind if she played a song for us on the old piano in the dining room. We said we'd love to hear it. Brooke then played and sang "I Will Remember You," by Sarah McLachlan. When she finished, there wasn't a dry eye in the room.

Sheri's and Brooke's visit had a powerful effect on me. Not only had Brooke provided comfort and courage for me as I lay paralyzed and helpless, she also consoled and gave strength to Sheri once she arrived at the accident site. Now, eighteen days later, the three of us were here together under far different circumstances enjoying the abundance of blessings being showered upon us.

A TRIP TO THE GROCERY STORE

Near the end of my second week of inpatient rehab, Avi decided I was ready for what he called "comprehensive integration." He announced this by saying, "Hey, John, let's walk across the street and go shopping at the grocery store."

"That's funny, Avi. What are we really going to do?"

"John, I'm not kidding. I want you to experience leaving the hospital grounds, crossing the street, and navigating the grocery store as if you were going to pick up a few items for dinner."

"Sounds kind of interesting. Whatever you say, Avi. Let's give it a go."

So we left my room and headed out the front of the hospital. A short walk brought us to the traffic light-controlled, four-way intersection. Crossing the street would put us into the grocery store parking lot.

Avi pressed the crosswalk button on the light pole. Once we got the go-ahead indicator, we needed to step off the curb and cross the street. There was just one problem—I froze in my tracks. I looked left, then right, then left, then right again. I suddenly realized every car looked like a clear and present danger to me. This was the first time since the accident that I had interacted with moving cars. I am not a psychologist, but I think it would be reasonable to say that some degree of post-traumatic stress syndrome had reared its ugly head.

Avi immediately sensed and recognized my reaction. He asked me if I was all right and assured me that it was okay to cross. Using him as a guide and as another set of eyes and ears, we proceeded to cross safely. Once on the other side, we made our way up the parking lot entrance, and then I saw her coming right at me.

I yelled out to Avi, "She's going to run me over!" It wasn't a car. It was someone on a bicycle coming out of the parking lot. Her front brake cable had snapped, and she panicked. It caught her by surprise so much that she had forgotten about her rear brake. Clearly, she was not an experienced cyclist. Her bike was headed right for me. Every time I dodged left or right to avoid her, she seemed to change direction and headed directly toward my center mass.

All I could think of was how ironic this was. Just nineteen days ago, I almost lost my life and was rendered paralyzed from below my neck having been struck by a car while riding my bike. Now, after two successful surgeries and a miraculous recovery, I was about to get whacked by a runaway bike ridden by a novice cyclist. Are you kidding me?

Avi knew the cyclist's name and kept yelling at her to use both brakes. Finally, his voice penetrated her panic. She squeezed hard on the rear brake, and the bike came to a stop about ten feet in front of me. I just shook my head in total disbelief.

The rest of the outing was uneventful. Crossing at the light on our return caused me much less anxiety. I think I was still in shock from the trip over. By the time we were back in my room, Avi and I were laughing off the whole incident. We both agreed that I had been spared and healed, after being hit by a car, for a purpose a little higher than to be run over by a rogue cyclist.

HIGH WATER MARK

Thursday, September 10, the day before my discharge, my physical and occupational therapists wanted to be sure I was ready for re-entry into my home environment. So shortly after breakfast, Avi was back in my room to do his part. There is a saying in sports: practice doesn't make perfect; perfect practice makes perfect. Avi was keen to make doubly certain I could handle showers, grooming, and dressing safely and successfully. For the next hour, I did all of these under his watchful eye. After finishing them, he gave me two thumbs up.

Next, I geared up for physical therapy at 9:00 a.m. with therapist Dani. When she came to my room to get me, her greeting was a bit puzzling.

"We are going to go outside today, John. How would you like to see the ocean?"

Caught completely off guard, I said, "What do you mean, in a car?"

"That's funny, John. No, we're going to walk. It's less than a quarter of a mile to the top of the hill. You can see it from there."

"Dani, I haven't seen the ocean in twenty days. You know, the last time was just moments before the accident. Yeah, I'd love to go see it."

We headed out the front of the hospital toward the intersection involved in yesterday's excursion to the grocery store. It was a spectacular morning with not a hint of clouds or marine layer. This time, we didn't cross the street, but turned right and followed the sidewalk up the hill heading west toward the ocean. After walking over 1,000 feet, a distance beyond my wildest dreams two weeks ago, we arrived at the crest and stopped. As the morning sun shone on the endless horizon, there it was in all its glory—the Pacific Ocean. It radiated a royal blue as gently rolling waves played tag with the low-flying pelicans. I could smell the salty air just as I had done the day of my fateful ride. I took a very deep breath and tried to capture the memory. Dani stood by me, quietly, and allowed me to experience the serenity of the moment. I felt awash in grace—so lucky, so blessed.

My PT and OT teams had done their jobs to perfection. I was ready to be discharged, ahead of schedule. I would be home in time to celebrate my birthday.

GOING HOME

The excitement of being discharged and going home made sleep the night before almost impossible, so I wandered the hallway, socializing with the night staff. Strolling down to the nurses' station to visit and raiding the refrigerator for pudding had become a nightly ritual. I thoroughly enjoyed visiting with the staff during the wee hours of the morning when things were slower for them. It gave me a chance to get to know everyone better. Most of the staff, especially those assigned to my team, seemed like extended family to me. I knew the feeling might fade after being discharged, so I wanted to enjoy the connections while they lasted.

Finally, I got a few hours rest and was up again by 5:15 a.m. Before showering, I headed out to the courtyard one last time. I had gone there almost every morning before breakfast during the past two weeks to pray and to prepare myself for the day ahead. At first, my visits to it were in my wheelchair. Eventually, I was able to walk to the courtyard, sit down on a bench amidst the cool morning air, and marvel at the gift I had been given.

Friday, September 11, would be no different. Stepping outside, I was greeted by the scents of the summer flowers and enveloped by gentle rays from a gorgeous sunrise. I gazed upward and watched a layer of wispy clouds turn from a brilliant red, to orange, to pink, and finally, to a soft, pale white. "This is going to be a great day," I whispered to myself.

I had asked Sheri to bring in one of my favorite Specialized™ riding jerseys the day before, which seemed fitting to wear on this day. I'd lost so much weight, it draped on me as if I were a hanger. I would need to do a lot of work to get back the muscle mass I had lost during the last three weeks. Still, I was eternally grateful to have the chance.

Sheri, Meg, and Wes were busy completing last-minute preparations to get our home ready for me, so I wouldn't see them until mid-morning. The rehabilitation center team had been adamant about certain things (such as handrails in our shower) that had to be in place before I was released. It was just as well. I needed the time to say "thank you" to as many people as I could find.

To help celebrate my discharge day, Sheri brought a large rectangular carrot cake to feed forty-eight people. A standing joke during my two-week inpatient stay was that the carrot cake in the cafeteria was always "sold out" by the time I asked for it. We took the cake into the dining room and invited everyone in the rehab unit to come by and get a piece. Hugs and high-fives were shared with everyone that came. It felt like Sheri, Meg, Wes, and I were celebrating my discharge day with a very large family, which is really what the rehab staff had become during my two-week stay. We even managed lots of group pictures—with people on my team and throughout the unit. It was a very happy and joyous morning.

A bit of housekeeping was in order, though. Everything in Room 151A needed to be packed and moved to the car. Meg and Wes were real troopers and managed to collect all of my things. One item I asked them not to pack was my small whiteboard, which resided on the wall opposite the end of my bed. I wanted to carry it to the car myself. Victoriously using my right hand, I managed to print the following message on it:

JOHN'S
DAY 21/14

It signified the twenty-first day since my horrific accident and the fourteenth day of my stay in the rehabilitation center. During those three weeks, I had survived a devastating and complete spinal cord injury, which left me paralyzed from below the neck. A young, brilliant, and talented neurosurgeon and his team performed emergent spine surgery and gave me another chance at life. My right vertebral artery had been embolized to stop the blood flow using cutting edge techniques, eliminating the possibility of a blood clot traveling to my brain and causing a massive stroke, or worse, death. I began to heal in the SICU. Then, after seven days, I was transferred to the rehab center, arriving on a gurney with an IV, catheter, nose tube, and neck brace. The last fourteen days as a rehabilitation inpatient had been a whirlwind.

My miraculous recovery from total paralysis was well on its way, but not yet complete. It would take many months of outpatient rehabilitation and a personal commitment to physical conditioning on my own to recover 100%.

The focus today, though, was about celebrating an end to the most amazing three weeks of my life. As is their custom when discharging a patient, the staff gathered by the nurses' station and cheered while ringing a bell to announce another successful patient departure. With my neck brace properly positioned, we said our final good-byes and began the short walk toward the front door and outside to our waiting car.

Holding Sheri's hand firmly within my own, I knew there was nothing more I needed to get me home—no wheelchair, no walker, no cane.

PART IV

THE CIRCLE IS NOW COMPLETE

OUTPATIENT REHABILITATION

The day after I came home, Saturday, September 12, our son Matt made a surprise visit (at least to me) from Virginia. He had been in constant communication with Sheri and Meg from the moment he was told about my accident. Once transferred to the rehab center, Matt and I spoke almost every day. He and Sheri had decided early on that his time away from work would be best spent to come to Carlsbad and join in my birthday celebration and to help her with my transition to being home. Now that I was there in time for my birthday, I enjoyed his week-long visit all the more.

Nevertheless, reentry into life at home was not as easy as I had thought it would be. Yes, it was fantastic to be out of hospital and rehab center environments, once again, surrounded with my own familiar belongings. However, it became all too clear very quickly how little strength and stamina I had. Finding a comfortable position in bed for sleeping seemed to elude me, no matter what I tried to do. Ironically, and similar to what I had experienced in the rehab center, the major source of my pain was my damaged shoulder, not my neck. An

MRI would soon determine if surgery, rehabilitation, or a combination of the two would be the proper course of action.

As soon as we could get it scheduled, I started going to Scripps Memorial Hospital Encinitas Rehabilitation Center as an outpatient. In addition to receiving great care, each appointment gave me the opportunity to say hello to the wonderful professionals who helped me to heal enough to be discharged and go home. The first two months were focused working on my right arm and shoulder with physical therapist, Lee Ann. The exercises were intended to help stimulate surrounding muscle groups and to promote neural pathway healing. To augment this treatment, I was doing exercises at home diligently and stretching on my own several times a day. Sheri and I walked every day, too. First, it was one-half mile strolls around our neighborhood park. Within a month or so, we were clocking two miles every day, keeping a slow but steady pace.

Still, my shoulder pain persisted, so a follow-up with the orthopedic surgeon, Dr. Nichols, was high on my list. Just one month from the accident date, he ordered the much-needed MRI for my right shoulder. It was time to get a better look inside to determine if the rotator cuff was torn.

Unexpectedly, when I was being slid into the MRI tube, I had a flashback to the brief moment when I awoke in the MRI tube in the trauma center thirty days prior. I'd been paralyzed back then and had totally suppressed that memory until now. It took everything I had to avoid pushing the red panic button, which would have aborted the shoulder MRI. I kept telling myself that if I didn't get it done today, I would have to come back and try again. I began saying the rosary in my head. I knew it would take me about the same amount of time to finish as it would to conduct the MRI. It worked.

Results of the test were encouraging; I did not have a rotator cuff tear, but the impingement syndrome remained. Getting better would require a great deal of physical rehabilitation, but I was committed to do whatever it took. Achieving a normal, active lifestyle was within my reach. If being able to do all of the things I did before the accident meant I needed to invest a great deal of sweat equity, I was all in.

Once the calendar flipped to 2010, it was time for more challenging therapies. Anne, my new physical therapist, got much more aggressive with my upper body. She finally worked out a leftover knot under my right scapula. Diane, my occupational therapist, worked her magic on my right wrist and right hand. She increased my squeeze strength and dexterity substantially. Eventually, I was able to write cursive legibly again and sign my name. All of this supervised rehabilitation continued to be augmented by my workouts at home.

My neck brace had been removed near the end of October 2009. One day in February 2010, I decided it was time to get back on my bike and set aside residual angst and fear leftover from last August. I began to mount my bike for very easy spins on the indoor trainer. Gradually, I added more minutes and higher gears. As the rest of my body became stronger, especially my neck muscles, I was able to increase my workouts on the bike to one hour at a time. It seemed as though every revolution I made on the bike took me further away from any anxiety I had about cycling. Awful memories were being replaced with a newfound zeal for the sport, which soon turned into an idea for a celebration.

By the middle of March, my five-month, medically supervised, and quite successful outpatient rehabilitation came to an end. However, it did not mark the end of my self-managed workouts. I added light weights, more time on my bike trainer, and cross-training on my NordicTrack. Combined with walking and stretching, slowly and steadily, my body got stronger, and physical activity of every kind became more natural. Finally, one day in April, while walking back to our car with a shopping cart of items from Costco, I looked at Sheri and said, "I'm going to see if I can jog while pushing this cart." To date, the best pace I had achieved was a brisk walk.

"Be *absolutely* certain you keep your hands on that cart and watch out for moving cars!" she said quite sternly. Sheri had almost lost me and wasn't about to see me give back all the gains with some parking lot stunt.

I knew it wasn't a stunt, though, and I knew my limitations. With a little extra push, I broke from a comfortable walk into a very slow jog. I could feel my body saying to me, "Hey, what's this? I haven't done this in a long time. It feels really good!" And so it did.

Soon, I graduated from the Costco cart-assisted jogs to doing intermittent fifty-yard sprints during our walks in the park. The first time I did one of those, I'm not sure who was more shocked, Sheri or me.

From there, it just got better. I no longer thought about keeping my balance when I walked, jogged, or navigated stairs. I drove a car without wondering if every other car on the road was trying to hit me. I could swivel my head with a greater degree of movement. When we traveled, I handled the luggage. When we grocery shopped, I carried the bags into the house. I took showers without the assistance of a chair. I could eat meals using either hand and tie my shoes effortlessly. Loud, spontaneous laughter returned, as did the ability to be intimate with Sheri. Through a combination of medical intervention, a miracle, and self-motivation, my recovery was almost complete.

THE CELEBRATION RIDE

By early May, I had built up my cycling endurance to about 40 percent of my pre-accident ability and was improving rapidly. Even so, it was the indoor trainer type of endurance, which is quite different from what is needed for outdoor road conditions.

Then, I had an idea. There were two organizations I particularly wanted to thank, Scripps Health (Scripps) and UnitedHealthcare (UHC), for all they had done for me and my family. What if I could get them to sponsor a celebration bike ride to draw attention to how they had helped me in a desperate time of need?

I kicked the idea around with Mike Godfrey, a senior director of marketing at Scripps, who seemed to like it. Soon thereafter, I had a chance encounter with Kathlyn Wee, a VP for UHC, at a trade show in Chicago which I attended annually with Sheri. I told her my story and what I wanted to do with the ride. Kathlyn immediately got the ball rolling. Her efforts led me to her boss, Bill Whitely, UHC's Chief Growth Officer at the time, and ultimately Dave Anderson, UHC's CEO for Southern California. Incidentally, Dave was instrumental in creating and managing their sponsorship of the UnitedHealthcare Pro Cycling Team.

Once I had Scripps' and UHC's commitment, only one piece of the puzzle was missing—I needed to get back on my bike on the road. This was much easier said than done. First, I needed a road-worthy bike. While mine was safe for an indoor trainer, the damage to the carbon-fiber frame made it unsafe for road conditions. Fortunately, a local bike shop, B&L Bikes, loaned me a brand-new Specialized™ Roubaix.

The second step, actually venturing out on the road among cars, was much tougher, at least mentally and emotionally. I started by riding in and around the parking lot of our neighborhood park. From there, I progressed to riding the hilly streets near our home. It took weeks to become even remotely comfortable riding in a bike lane among cars. To be honest, I will never feel safe again with cars around, especially with the explosion of smartphone functionality. Too many drivers with too many self-imposed distractions does not bode well for unprotected cyclists. Thank goodness, many cities have a variety of well-protected bike trails. In the end, I managed to train outdoors safely and was confident that I was ready for the event.

After several months of planning, all the pieces came together. Scripps and UHC sponsored the "Celebration Ride" from Scripps Memorial Hospital La Jolla to Scripps Memorial Hospital Encinitas Rehabilitation Center on August 27, 2010. We would be riding on the eve of my one-year anniversary of my transfer between the two hospitals. Some of the staff from the Scripps hospitals, including three of my physical therapists and the CEO of Scripps Memorial Hospital Encinitas, Carl Etter, joined me for the ride. From UHC, we had Dave Anderson and Tom Donham, a VP who worked for Dave.

As a major bonus and a thrill I will never forget, Dave arranged for the captain of the UHC Pro Cycling Team, Rory Sutherland (as of this writing, he rides for Team Tinkoff-Saxo), to ride with us. For you golfers out there, think playing eighteen holes with Phil Mickelson. How cool would that be?

Rory was absolutely gracious and his wife, Cheynna, an accomplished competitive cyclist in her own right, also joined the ride. It was an event I will never forget. Scripps and UHC were generous beyond any expectation, and UHC produced a one-of-a-kind jersey for me to wear for the ride. It has become, without a doubt, my favorite jersey! Thierry Attias, president of Millennium Sports, augmented the jersey with the rest of the cycling kit (socks, bib, jacket, hat, etc.). I felt like a million bucks!

Before we set out on our short fourteen-mile ride from La Jolla to Encinitas, a crowd had gathered and some people important to my recovery offered some thoughts about what had happened to me and why we were taking this ride. When Dr. Leary made his remarks, it was difficult for me to not get choked up. Thanks to him and many others, I was about to be on the road again.

As our small peloton left the Scripps Memorial Hospital La Jolla parking lot, I had to force myself to take deep breaths. I felt like I was in a fantasy world. As we began a slow climb up the very steep Genesis hill, my heart was racing. I kept thinking about how unbelievable it was to be doing this ride after coming so close to a life in a wheelchair.

Once we arrived at the top of the hill, we made a right turn onto the Pacific Coast Highway and headed north. Passing Torrey Pines golf course, we zoomed down the backside of the Torrey Pines hill and the state park. By now, we were going between 35 and 40 mph. For an amateur cyclist who had experienced quadriplegia, I can assure you that my adrenaline was pumping big time. As we rode through Del Mar, Rory commented on how many times he had used this route during training rides and how dangerous it seemed to be. So our peloton "became a car" and took the entire width of the north-bound lane until we exited the downtown area.

From there, we headed into the open along PCH with the Pacific Ocean in full view on our left. As my lungs filled with the salty air, my mind was spinning with a mixture of memories from safer rides along this route and of the events of the last year. That lemonade I promised myself about a year earlier in the shower in the rehab center was beginning to be made.

Coincidentally, Scripps Memorial Hospital Encinitas was having an all-day "spirit rally" on the twenty-seventh, where a lively combination of food and success stories were being shared. I knew Mike Godfrey had arranged for a finish line greeting there, but I hardly expected what I found when we arrived.

Hundreds of employees of Scripps lined the makeshift finish line in the parking lot holding banners of encouragement, cheering at the top of their lungs.

My fellow riders gave me the win, letting me cross the finish line first. As I slowly came to a stop about twenty yards away, I unclicked my left pedal, dropped down over my handlebars, and lost it. I was simply and completely overcome with emotion and memories of the past year.

Once I gathered myself together, I turned and headed back to the crowd, where I immediately recognized the people who nursed, coached, and trained me back to health. Sheri was the first person to give me a hug. Staff from my rehab team hung celebratory strings of beads around my neck. Everyone was clapping, cheering, and smiling. Their reception filled me with so much joy and thankfulness. Fortunately, Mike recorded most of the ride and finish-line celebration so Sheri and I can relive that magnificent day every year.

Many wonderful people from Scripps and UHC contributed to the success of the "Celebration Ride." However, there was one person who I noticed immediately—Chris Garcia, the man who had called 911 while running to give me aid at the accident scene. Unbeknownst to me, Sheri had called Chris to let him know about the event. We had seen Chris shortly after my discharge to thank him for what he had done for me, but we had not connected with him since. It was great to have him and his wife there. I was so excited; I decided to introduce him to the press reporters who were covering the event.

"This is Chris Garcia," I said grinning ear-to-ear. He saw the impact and was the first citizen responder to come to my aid and to call 911!"

No doubt this was the coolest fourteen-mile bike ride I had ever taken and probably ever will.

SHARING THE SHIRTS

One very early morning near the end of my first week in the rehab center, I awoke, inspired. So many people had done so much to help me and my family to get to that point in my recovery, and we knew more were helping every day. I felt strongly that they had to be properly thanked. As I lay in my bed, I came up with the idea for a very special polo shirt—red for the women and navy for the men. It took no time at all to figure out what I wanted embroidered on the sleeves. The left one would read "8/21/09" and the right one "John's Team." Now, what to put on the left front? I kept thinking about what Dr. Leary had called me, "Miracle Boy." From that, I derived "Part of a Miracle," and so it was.

I collected as many names of people (and their shirt sizes) who had contributed to my recovery as I could, both in the La Jolla hospital and the rehabilitation center in Encinitas. Sheri and I began to estimate how many others there would be, including the citizen responders, paramedics, flight crew, support staff, family, and friends. Ultimately, we placed an order for 200 shirts.

A few weeks after my discharge from the rehabilitation center, the shirts arrived at our home. Sheri and I began our efforts to track down as many people as we could find who had contributed to my recovery. Family and friends received the first batch, and the rest, a total of 152 shirts, were given to all of the citizen responders and the unsung medical heroes who do an incredibly selfless and professional job every day. Theirs is truly a worthy calling.

While we enjoyed gifting all of the shirts, several occasions stood out. The first was when we presented Dr. Leary his shirt at my thirty-day follow-up visit. Just a little over a month prior, he was counseling Sheri and me on how remote my chances were of even a slight recovery—and now this. You would have thought we had given him a new Porsche.

The second shirt-gifting involved the Mercy Air flight crew. They remembered the accident and graciously spent an hour hosting Sheri and me at their flight headquarters, including a tour of the helicopter which transported me to the trauma center. Looking inside at all of the medical equipment was somewhat surreal. Immediately, I had flashbacks of looking down at my seemingly lifeless body, unable to move it or feel it. Right away, Sheri sensed what was happening.

"Are you okay?" she asked.

"Yeah, I'm okay. In fact, I couldn't be better."

We hugged each other, took more group photos with the flight crew, and thanked them from the bottom of our hearts for what they did that day.

What fun it was to give Dr. Tominaga her red polo shirt. She beamed as though she had just received her perfect Christmas gift. It was only fitting that Sheri took a picture of Dr. T and me standing together in front of the SICU "wall of miracles."

We also paid a surprise visit to Chris Van Gorder, President and CEO of Scripps Health. When Sheri and I arrived unannounced at the Scripps Corporate Headquarters, Chris was not quite sure what to make of our impromptu visit. Virginia, his executive assistant, was sent to greet us to get clarity as to the purpose of our visit. As soon as we told her my story and learned that we were there to present Chris with a shirt as a thank you for the entire Scripps organization, Virginia summoned him to the lobby to meet us. What joy Sheri and I got that day to see his reaction to our gift and to hear the sincerity in his voice as he thanked us.

Finally, Sheri and I caught up with Dr. Pettit and Peter Schultz, the nurse practitioner who assisted Dr. Leary during my C5-C6 ACDF spine surgery. Dr. Pettit jokingly remarked about how prescient he was in predicting my total recovery. Peter enjoyed describing some of the details of my surgery and reminded us how lucky I was to have had Dr. Leary as my neurosurgeon. We quickly agreed.

As a result of researching and writing this book, I realized there are some people who we overlooked in our shirt distribution. It will give Sheri and me a great deal of pleasure to find them all and to present them with their very own "Part of a Miracle" polo shirt. It is never too late to say thank you.

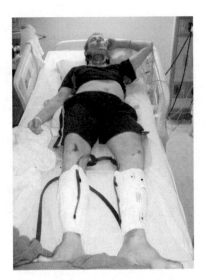

8/30/09—Resting in rehabilitation room 151A with sequential compression devices, or sequentials, to prevent Deep Vein Thrombosis (DVT)

Rehab center 'discharge day' 9/11/09; Wes, Meg, me, and Sheri

9/11/09 surrounded by some of the great staff at the rehabilitation center

After 21 days since the accident, the last 14 days in the rehab center, I'm headed home four days early (notice my right hand fingers; neural pathways were still healing)

Back home—Matt, Sheri, me, Meg, and Wes

Brooke gets her 'John's Team' shirt

Time-out from outpatient rehab for a photo with some rehab center staff in their 'John's Team' shirts

Dr. Gail Tominaga (Dr. T) and me in the trauma center. Sheri and I just gave her a red 'John's Team' shirt

Peter Schultz, NP, me, and Dr. Jim Pettit,
anesthesiologist, having just been given their
navy 'John's Team' shirts by me and Sheri

Authors together on 10/22/09 in Dr. Leary's office
the day my neck brace came off for good!

Mercy Air crew with me at their Carlsbad, CA base; they kept me alive and stabilized while flying me 30 miles south to the Scripps Memorial Hospital La Jolla (SMH-LJ) trauma center

Surgical team members Jimmy Catalma, RN (far left) and Joseph Valenta, ORT (far right) with Dr. Leary and Gary Fybel (in navy John's Team shirt), CEO of SMH-LJ, at the ride send-off

Sheri giving me a 'good luck' hug just before the start of the 'Celebration Ride'; my jersey is a one-of-a-kind!

Dave Anderson (UnitedHealthcare CEO SoCal), me, Rory Sutherland (UHC ProCycling Team; now rides for Team Tinkoff-Saxo), and Tom Donham (UnitedHealthcare VP) just before we 'clicked in' to start the ride

left to right: Rory Sutherland, me, and Carl Etter (CEO Scripps Memorial Hospital Encinitas and Rehabilitation Center) leading the way at the start of the 'Celebration Ride'

'Celebration Ride' peloton heads north on Pacific Coast Highway

Me crossing the finish line of the 'Celebration Ride' at Scripps Memorial Hospital Encinitas

First post-ride hug from Sheri

Some of the staff greeting the peloton as
we crossed the finish line

Receiving congratulations from occupational
therapist, Avi Kouzi

Never a dull moment with fellow rider and physical therapist, James (Jim) Cope

Nurse Jackie and Nurse Aida wearing 'John's Team' shirts with me at the finish

Chris Garcia and his wife Stacey with me post-ride—
glad he called 911!

Meg, Liam (first grandchild and born on Sheri's
birthday), and me—November 2010

HEALING POWERS

Since my accident and recovery, I have had the pleasure of telling my story to many people. Whether it's in a five-minute, one-on-one conversation, or a forty-five-minute presentation to hundreds of medical professionals, listeners react to it by describing my story as amazing, incredible, astonishing, encouraging, and inspirational.

People are stunned by both my miraculous recovery and the speed with which it occurred. Then, after listeners get past their initial reactions, they tend to ask me the same two questions: What was your source of strength? Why do you think this happened to you?

Regarding the first question, I am hardly the first person to face an extreme medical situation with seemingly insurmountable odds. I do know, as do many others, the idea of giving up and giving in to my circumstance was never an option. Yet without lots of strength and inspiration, there was no way I could have recovered fully. I described my sources for these as Healing Powers: the Power of Faith and Prayer, the

Power of the Human Spirit, and the Power of Family and Friends.

The Power of Faith and Prayer influenced my outcome from the very beginning. Immediately, after I was impacted by the car and landed on the road, the pain I experienced was so excruciating, my mind could focus on nothing else. However, once paralysis took hold and I was overcome with fear, I began to lean heavily on my faith in God. Lying on my back, utterly helpless and motionless, praying was the only thing I knew I could still do. I began saying the Hail Mary repeatedly and asking for God's help in what was my most desperate hour.

Praying gave me strength, courage, hope, and the peace of mind to accept the outcome, whatever it might be. Staring directly into the face of two unwanted possibilities, quadriplegia or death, my faith and my prayers had a way of turning the tables on my dire situation.

And of course, I wasn't the only person praying. Sheri, Meg, and Wes began praying as soon as they were notified of my accident. They continued to pray together when they first arrived in the trauma center waiting room. Also, while I was in the SICU, multiple global prayer circles for my healing and recovery were formed within days. One was initiated by Meg and Wes, through their affiliation with Campus Crusade for Christ, and another by the hospital chaplain, who was amazed at the swiftness with which his was formed.

When my right hand lagged so far behind in recovery, Meg sent out a specific prayer request to her network of friends, family, and supporters, asking them to pray for it to heal. It did.

Armed with the knowledge that others were praying for me, combined with my own faith, the Power of *my* Human Spirit became supercharged. This power gave me the will to live, and then, the will to recover. It was with me at the accident scene when I realized I was paralyzed, but I was not ready to die. It remained with me while I was in the trauma center, the SICU, inpatient rehabilitation, and throughout months of outpatient rehabilitation and self-directed physical training. Sure, it would have been easy to give up and despair, but early on, I adopted an attitude that the only acceptable goal would be a 100% recovery.

I saw no reason to aim for anything less (even though I could find no documentation of a similar case of recovery). To achieve what I wanted, I had to believe such a recovery was possible, so I surrounded myself with people who had the same belief and had a positive, can-do, glass-half-full attitude. I pushed myself as far as I could go with every therapy session. If I thought my sessions could be more demanding, I asked the occupational and physical therapists to make them so. I wanted desperately to morph my new unpleasant reality back into the one I knew before the accident. However, to achieve the full potential of the Power of my Human Spirit, I needed help from other sources besides myself.

That energizing, external source came from the Power of Family and Friends. It would be nice to say that I maintained a positive mental attitude and had unshakeable faith throughout this amazing recovery, but I'm only human, and at times, I faltered. Whenever I did, my family, most notably my wife, Sheri, stood steadfastly by my side and infused me with their strength.

At times, if it became necessary, my family was willing to give me some tough love and a well-intentioned metaphorical kick in the pants. The outpouring of love from my family helped me to persevere during dark and discouraging times and to celebrate during bright and encouraging ones.

Friends played a part in fueling my human spirit, too. Whether I had known them for many years or for just a few months, they showered me with positive messages, encouragement, and prayers, all of which made a substantial impact on me and influenced my outcome.

While these three Healing Powers were my source of strength and inspiration, I would be remiss to not describe another critical component I needed to achieve a complete recovery—exceptional medical care. Without the support from San Diego County's Trauma System and Scripps Health's world-class medical care, I could have languished for days without proper diagnosis and state-of-the-art treatment. Without the education, training, and confidence of Dr. Leary and his willingness to proceed immediately with spine surgery, my outcome most likely would have resulted in quadriplegia. Recent staff additions, interventional neuro-radiologists Drs. Barr and Ammirati, helped me by eliminating the possibility of a massive stroke, or death, by performing cutting-edge surgery to embolize my right vertebral artery. Numerous other doctors, nurses, and technicians contributed along the way. And finally, an amazing team of occupational and physical therapists helped to assure my full recovery and complete return to the active daily living I enjoyed before the accident.

With their help, I have been given the chance to live out my life with meaning and purpose. I have also been given the time to contemplate the second question: Why do you think this happened to you?

I found my answer to be simple and inextricably linked with my faith—it was God's plan. I believe that he has a higher purpose for all of us. By surviving this tragic accident and recovering completely, I am able to bear witness to his miracle. It is my way to fulfill his divine plan.

The moment I was struck head on by the car on that beautiful August afternoon began the journey of my miraculous recovery from total paralysis. Also, it began a longer and more meaningful journey—a journey to give hope to people who have enormous challenges, to inspire researchers and philanthropists to continue their search for a cure for paralysis, and to remind healthcare professionals how lucky we are for their talent and dedication.

UNEXPECTED GIFTS

Throughout my ordeal, I was showered with so many gifts, but not the kind you open on Christmas or your birthday. Rather, these are gifts that make a lasting impression on your mind and in your heart. There is no unit of measure by which to gauge their worth. While it is not an exhaustive list or in any particular order, I wanted to share some of these gifts with you:

- Being free from paralysis and totally recovered
- Regaining my strength, agility, and coordination
- Learning how to forgive better
- Learning how to thank better
- Learning how to love better
- Learning how much I am loved
- Being able to share more life with my wife and best friend, Sheri
- Experiencing the love and support of Meg and Wes

- Celebrating the birth of my first grandchild, Liam
- Celebrating the birth of his baby sister, Lily
- Getting to talk with, see, and hug my son, Matt, and his wife, Kelly
- Celebrating the birth of their first child, Naya
- Having my faith renewed and my purpose clarified
- Reconnecting with my brother and three sisters on a more personal level
- Being able to cycle, play golf, and enjoy active daily living with no restrictions
- Developing a new appreciation for my entire family
- Understanding what is really important in life and what is not
- Cherishing my long-held friendships
- Creating new and lasting friendships and bonds
- Confirming the importance of giving back
- Being able to enjoy even more fully the gift of giving
- Attaining a deeper understanding of the power of prayer
- Learning to appreciate what I have and where I am in life

- Possessing a deep and lasting empathy for spinal cord injury patients

- Appreciation for what it means to be disabled

- Grasping a new understanding of the fragility and preciousness of life

- Realizing I have been given a chance to help others

Whenever I'm asked how the accident has affected me, my response is always the same. I explain that life's mysteries and ambiguities are no longer as perplexing to me. Also, I have more clarity as to my purpose in life—to bear witness to this miracle God has bestowed upon me. Then, I share with them the gift of a new perspective I have been given, expressed with six simple words: "Every day is a bonus day!"

EPILOGUE

One of my recovery goals included being able to play golf again. During the summer of 2010, I decided it was time to get serious. My first reentry to the sport was a baby step—a trip to the practice range to hit a medium-sized bucket of balls. I began with a wedge, and out of the first thirty balls, I must have shanked twenty of them.

If you're unfamiliar with the term *shanked*, it means you hit the ball with the hozzle of the club, where the shaft is attached to the club head, not the club head itself. This was not my objective. Instead of the ball launching into a high, arching 100-yard flight, it shot low to the ground at a nearly 45-degree angle. Luckily, I was at the end of the range, so no one was in danger of being hit by the golf balls I shanked that day.

I kept at it, though, and returned to the range again and again as my strength, my coordination, and my golf muscle memory began to improve. I knew Dr. Leary loved golf—he had become quite competitive and sported a single-digit handicap. The good doctor had invited me to play a round with him at his club when I thought I was ready. In February 2011, I decided it was time. Dr. Leary arranged for us to play on Saturday, February 5, amidst San Diego's gorgeous weather. It was incredible—in 2004, I'd been about a 3-handicap player. On that day, my score was well above 100, but I didn't care. In fact, I relished every stroke because I was doing another thing I thought I might never get to do ever again.

After the round, we rolled up to the clubhouse to off-load our clubs. I told Dr. Leary, rather awkwardly, how much the round had meant to me and how much I had enjoyed the day, but for some reason, I couldn't find the proper phrase to summarize how I felt.

He did. Without hesitation, he looked at me and said, "John, the circle is now complete."

"Amen, brother. Amen!"

ABOUT THE AUTHOR

JOHN MIKSA

John's 25+ year career in business development and general management with companies such as GE, AMR Corporation, CSC, and Rackspace, culminated as a CEO for a small technology start-up. Afterwards, John pursued some life-long interests, including writing, competitive amateur golf, volunteering, and cycling. In July, 2009, he self-published his first book,

The Robot Syndrome: how to overcome it and provide uniquely HUMAN customer service. After his accident on August 21st, 2009, John devoted himself to recovering completely and achieved that goal within one year. Understanding the significance of his medical outcome, he began the effort to chronicle his traumatic and amazing story in his second book.

With the release of *LASTING IMPACT: My Miraculous Recovery From Total Paralysis*, John has become fully engaged as a speaker to share his amazing story and bear witness to the miracle he received. He is a member of the Tate Publishing Speakers Bureau. His unbelievable journey of recovery, enabled by medical and divine intervention, is a timeless story and sure to fascinate and inspire healthcare, faith-based, and general audiences for years to come.

John can be contacted through his website www.johnmiksa.com, LinkedIn, Facebook, or directly at jjmiksa@gmail.com.

SCOTT P. LEARY, M.D.

Dr. Scott P. Leary is a board certified neurosurgeon and practices with Senta Clinic in San Diego, California. His clinical practice and research focuses on the comprehensive care of spinal disorders including; spinal stenosis, degenerative disc disease, spinal trauma, scoliosis, failed spine surgery syndrome, spinal tumors and neck and back pain.

He obtained his medical degree from the prestigious Washington University in St. Louis, where his medical school class was ranked #1 in the United States. After residency, Dr. Leary completed two fellowships— the first in neurosurgery and the second in complex spine surgery. This unique combination makes him one of a very few neurosurgeons to have completed a neurosurgery residency and an orthopedic complex spine surgery fellowship.

Dr. Leary has received numerous honors, including selection as one of America's Top Surgeons by the

Consumers Research Council and a finalist for the Health Care Champion Award for Innovation and Research in San Diego by the San Diego Business Journal. He is active in clinical research studies and currently serves as a Principal Investigator for FDA regulated clinical trials for treatment of symptomatic degenerative disc disease and spinal stenosis.

Currently, he is the Chief of Spine Surgery Committee at Scripps Memorial Hospital-La Jolla and is affiliated with Scripps Memorial Hospital (La Jolla and Encinitas) and Sharp Grossmont Hospital, as well as with SMI Outpatient Surgery Center.

For more information please visit Dr. Leary's website, www.drscottleary.com.